ALCOHOLISM
ITS SCOPE,
CAUSE AND TREATMENT

Alcoholism

ITS SCOPE,
CAUSE AND TREATMENT

Ruth Fox, M.D. & *Peter Lyon*

RANDOM HOUSE / NEW YORK

FIFTH PRINTING, JUNE 1966

Published in New York by Random House, Inc., and
simultaneously in Toronto, Canada, by Random House
of Canada, Limited.

Library of Congress Catalog Card Number: 55-8170

Manufactured in the United States of America

CONTENTS

27420

Introduction

A prodigious amount of emotion and thought has been invested in the questions raised by alcohol and alcoholism. Emotionally, we are all of us ranged on one or the other side of the broader question, whether we want to be or not: the mere act of accepting or refusing a drink in one sense makes us partisan. As for the narrower question, that of the disease, it has been the subject, as its students are fond of pointing out, of books and articles to the number of more than one hundred thousand. The thought of all this material, its sheer bulk, is calculated to impress, and indeed it seems an awesome total. But there is nothing particularly startling about the size of this literature, except perhaps that it is so small. It is bound to be big and to grow bigger, and for two reasons.

In the first place, one cannot, when tackling alcoholism, focus solely on medical problems, as one can with other diseases, like cancer, the nature of which is imperfectly known. Alcoholism is primarily a disorder involving human behavior, and so its problems spill over into the fields of law and criminology, of government and politics, of religion, morality, and ethics, of anthropology, sociology, history, economics, and education. Even such medical matters as the cause, treatment, and conjectural cure of alcoholism must be related to these other fields; and the clinician must keep pace with the work being done by specialists in each of these other fields on the problems posed by the use of alcohol. The crucial contribution to our knowledge can come from any one of these other disciplines. And so the literature proliferates.

Moreover, we know, at present, so little. The swamp of our ignorance is hedged about densely with confusion, complexity, contradiction, and contention. Within, under the guise of objective fact, is to be found personal opinion, arbitrary judgment, evasion, prejudice, polemic, and out-and-out myth. It is just the sort of wilderness calculated to attract the scientific explorer, and it is no wonder that he has come here, especially in the last generation, by the hundreds. What he is up against can be suggested by posing four very basic questions:

What is drunkenness?

It will not avail to turn to the largest, most inclusive dictionary, where all one will find, as explanation, will be such terms as *intoxication* and *inebriety*. Synonyms are not wanting, nor are equivalents in slang (of which there must be at least a hundred in the English language alone). But at what point is a person drunk? Which is to say, how much alcohol ingested constitutes drunkenness? In point of fact, there is no standard, no dividing line, except one that is wholly arbitrary and was established as recently as 1952. A Uniform Vehicle Code published by the Federal government in that year for the guidance of law enforcement officials urged that if the blood alcohol concentration by weight was less than 0.05 per cent the individual could be considered sober, if it was between 0.05 per cent and 0.15 per cent his condition would be questionable, and if it was above 0.15 per cent he could be considered legally under the influence. (For comparative reference, a blood alcohol concentration of 0.50 per cent can be fatal.)

But tolerance to alcohol varies. It varies from one individual to another in relation to a number of factors, and it varies in the same individual depending on still other factors (fatigue, psychological condition, food recently eaten, and so on) only some of which have any effect on the blood alcohol concentration. And tolerance is only one of the considerations that muddies the picture of what constitutes drunkenness.

After extensive tests conducted at Michigan State College in cooperation with the National Safety Council, the testing physiologists recommended that the Federal standards be revised and amplified like this: 0.00–0.05 per cent safe; 0.05–0.10 per cent possibly under the influence; 0.10–0.15 per cent probably under the influence; above 0.15 per cent definitely under the influence. After which they concluded: "It is recommended that additional study be devoted to clarification and understanding of the term 'intoxicated' for legal purposes." Which is to say, we still have not agreed.

What is alcoholism?

This question will be discussed in greater detail later on; for the moment, it suffices to say that there is disagreement as to how to define, classify, and diagnose alcoholism. Gather two dozen experts together for the purpose of stating scientifically what it is they are expert in, and you will quite likely be confronted with, if not as many definitions, at least half-a-dozen, each quite useful in its own way, but each differing from the others.

The use of alcohol brings about quite different results in different people: all of us have observed how this one will be gay, that one tearful; this one arrogant, that one sleepy; in fact, the same one individual may in the course of an evening go through two or more quite different stages. Similarly, the abuse of alcohol leads, with different people, to quite different reactions. Alcohol addicts, too, especially in the early stages of their addiction, may be affected quite differently.

It is difficult enough, then, to arrive at an inclusive definition that will describe the sickness for one culture (as, for instance, the multi-faceted culture of the United States), but even more difficult if the definition must cover, in addition, such wine-bibbing peoples as the French and the Italians.

In the summer of 1954, twenty-nine specialists in the field of alcoholism, representing the disciplines of pharmacology, biochemistry, physiology, psychology, psychiatry, anthropology, sociology, clinical medicine, and education, met in Toronto to attempt, among other things, a clarification of terminology. The definition which, they agreed, was perhaps the most useful reads: "A chronic disease, or disorder of behavior, characterized by the repeated drinking of alcoholic beverages to an extent that exceeds customary dietary use or ordinary compliance with the social drinking customs of the community, and that interferes with the drinker's health, interpersonal relations or economic functioning." But there is scarcely a clinician, psychiatrist, or sociologist who would not like to add to this statement, or weight some of its aspects, or scratch it out entirely and start fresh—based on his own experience.

What, then, is an alcoholic?

Again, there is an almost total confusion of terminology and, what is more important, of ideas underlying the terminology. Scientists characteristically attempt to extract generalizations

4

from a series of observations based on the data that come to their attention. Here the difficulty is that alcoholics as a group resist categorization. The only denominator common to each of them is that they drink alcoholic beverages. Qualifications of that statement—even phrases like *more than they should* or *too much* or *repeatedly* or *without control*—run into the danger threatening all generalizations about alcoholics: the evident alcoholic for whom there is no ready label. Nevertheless, there have been several careful and skilful attempts to classify alcoholics. Thus, terms like problem drinker, situational drinker, symptomatic drinker, primary addict, secondary addict, addictive drinker, regular symptomatic excessive drinker, irregular symptomatic excessive drinker, chronic inebriate, chronic alcoholic, and a dozen more have been used by various students of the sickness. One difficulty is that these terms change their meaning in the usage of various experts: what one clinician means by symptomatic drinker is quite different from what another means. Such semantic confusions are more than merely wasteful or irritating; they are roadblocks to fruitful research.

Proposals for terms to define degrees and varieties of dependence on alcohol will be offered later on, together with discussion of the terms most widely current. Two points should, however, be made now.

In the first place, the term *alcoholic* is itself encumbered with derogatory connotations. There is something unfortunately disparaging about it, due to the false insistence on the part of many of us, including indeed many physicians, that the alcoholic is perverse or weak-willed rather than truly sick and addictive. These moral strictures of course pervade all aspects of the subject, creating their own tiresome confusions.

The second point is this: to attempt to establish any discrete classifications whatever based on degrees and variations of addiction to alcohol is to court trouble. For there comes a point, both in the course of the alcoholic's sickness and in the experience of the trained diagnostician, when it seems idle to attempt to classify, to try to erect any hopeful set of distinctions. As far as the patient is concerned, one knows that he must stop drinking. As far as the diagnostician is concerned, gradations between, for example, primary and secondary addict, or regular and irregular symptomatic excessive drinker, lose their importance. When the distinctions become fuzzy for the diagnostician, a warning signal might well go up: he may be vulgarizing and oversimplifying. But not necessarily; it is characteristic of alcoholism that the distinctions between this and that category blur and disappear, after a time, that the symptoms merge and coincide. As the clinician tackles his, shall we say, thousandth case of alcoholism, he is no longer so concerned with the one of five or six or three classifications; he is concerned rather with the social recovery of the patient. To be sure, a differential diagnosis will be necessary for treatment; but just as there is no such thing as an uncomplicated case of addiction to alcohol, so there is no such thing as an uncomplicated course of treatment.

This is, of course, not to deny that the therapist's task might be appreciably eased by the establishment on a clear-cut basis of the varying degrees of addiction to alcohol and the varying abnormal reactions to alcohol. But it is to suggest that at the present there is no unanimity of opinion among the best qualified as to the number or extent of these variations. Obviously, it constitutes one of the most fruitful areas for further research.

How many alcoholics are there?

Where there is confusion about individual alcoholics, it might seem footling to attempt a census of the American population of alcoholics. Actually not, however: the confusion has to do with the classification of alcoholics. There would be little if any disagreement among qualified clinicians as to whether or not John Jones was an alcoholic. But unfortunately the fog creeps in again as soon as any attempt is made to estimate how widespread is the problem nationally. Here the confusion does not stem from disagreement among the experts, nor even so much from lack of competent research, although all will agree that much more extensive research must be undertaken. The trouble comes rather from the re-entry into the discussion of the emotional axe-grinders, the Wets and the Drys. For these well-organized groups, public opinion is a battleground, and each seeks to establish beachheads on which principles may be set up to guide our social behavior and determine our moral judgment.

Nowhere in the annals of medicine or public health has there been a sickness, a disorder, the course of which was so influenced or the treatment of which so compromised by social sanctions. For it is clear that, while alcohol is not *per se* the cause of alcoholism, there could be no alcoholics if there were no alcohol. Their characterological or biochemical flaws (whichever, or whichever combination, may be at the root of their sickness) might well result in some other disorder, but they could not be alcoholics. This truism suggests to the Drys that they should contend that the army of alcoholics is vast and growing and its onslaughts on the health of society mortal. There are even those Drys who will argue that alcoholism is the nation's number-one public health problem. To the Wets, contrariwise, there are many users of alcohol, but only a trivial, inconsiderable handful of abusers, among whom there are rare and exceptional individuals who are alcoholics. The impression is left that one can count them on the fingers of one hand.

It is foolish to expect that there will be any unanimity on the question so long as, on the one hand, there are highly

7

articulate, sincere, and passionately dedicated people who are convinced that the use of alcohol in any form is pernicious and sinful, and, on the other hand, some seventy million Americans who drink the product of an industry with a capital investment of nine billion dollars. Estimates of the number of American alcoholics, if polemics can be considered as reasonable appraisals, range all the way from less than 750,000 to more than 6,000,000 of us.

In the face of the assertions and counter-assertions, a formula has, however, been worked out, by Dr. E. M. Jellinek, * which takes into consideration several different factors: the number of deaths from cirrhosis of the liver, admissions to mental hospitals of alcoholic psychotics, arrests for drunkenness, admissions to general hospitals for diseases associated with chronic alcoholism, reports of deaths from alcoholism, and so on. Carefully weighted on the basis of experience, carefully checked against the results of occasional but limited field surveys, this formula indicates that there are in the United States between four and five million alcoholics.

To these should be added the habitual drunks: those who regularly drink to excess and are therefore in danger of becoming addicted to alcohol. In this group are those who, although not yet addictive drinkers, are a menace on the highways, a threat to the present and future of their families, often a public charge in the lock-ups, and usually a factor in absenteeism rates. They number between two and three million.

These totals are vague, but there is no way out of it. So long as stigmas attach to a sickness, case-finding must be hopelessly inadequate. Rather than being swiftly referred to a physician or clinic, the alcoholic, especially during the early sympto-

---

* Dr. Jellinek, presently consultant on alcoholism for the World Health Organization, was for many years associated with the Center of Alcohol Studies of Yale University.

matic stages of his drinking, is hidden and protected—by his own lies to himself and others, by his family, by his foreman, by his job associates. All concerned rebel at the notion that the individual is sick, is an alcoholic. And so public health authorities remain in the dark, and so the public health problem remains a question mark.

So far only four questions have been raised, the four to which, one would assume, the answers must surely have been found at the very outset of any program of study in the field. The point is, we are only just now at the outset of such a program; we have taken only a very few first steps; and any presumption that, if the answers to these four basic questions are still cloudy and disputed, comparable confusion and contradiction will attend every aspect of the subject, is well founded.

Nevertheless, along every one of the lines that lead to the central core of the problem, tangible progress has been made over the last generation. Three decades ago there were less than one hundred qualified clinicians specializing in alcoholism in the United States, probably fewer than one thousand in the entire world. But latterly, in the biochemistry, the metabolism, the endocrinology, and the physiological effects of alcohol, in nutrition, in the pharmacology of dozens of drugs used in the course of therapy, in sociological studies of drinking habits and effects—along a dozen exploratory avenues of research—science and medicine have been closing in on the unknown.

Hand-in-hand with the progress in research has come the more humane and intelligent approach to the inebriate and the alcoholic on the part of the churches, the courts and the law officials generally, the welfare agencies, industry and the trade unions—society. In nearly every state of the union some sort of program has been first legislated, then established on a pilot basis, and finally launched into action—action that includes treatment, research, and education. And if as yet the action is woefully weak, at least it has been started.

More important are the results of the work of the past generation in terms of human beings. Such matters cannot always be measured in terms of recovery statistics, dollars saved, days added to lives, marriage bonds strengthened, children restored to the security of love, traffic accidents avoided, commodities produced, or man-hours on the job; but they are nonetheless very real and very tangible, and they constitute the best reward for the clinician working in this field. Alcoholics have recovered by the scores of thousands. For some the period of recovery reaches back over ten, even twenty, years. Others, although not completely recovered, have at least gained sufficient insight into the nature of their conflicts so that they drink less, or less often, or at the very least, in such a way as to cause less distress to those around them. And, although this last may not seem to be a signal victory, it is; at the present stage of our knowledge, it is.

The present stage of our knowledge. The nub of it remains the sick individual. It is when we think of him, and puzzle over the causes, diagnosis, and treatment of his sickness, that the limitations of our knowledge become most obvious and most painful. It may be safely said, at this writing, that none can tell whether John Jones will become an alcoholic; that, if he already is, none can for a certainty tell why; that none can with assurance state that John Jones will recover from his alcoholism or that, if he does, for how long; and that, if he does recover for good, none will be able to say why, what aspect of his treatment did the trick.

The difficulty and the reach of the task can be stated simply enough. Most of us drink alcohol in one form or another. Some of us habitually drink too much of it, and this makes for one complex of problems. Others of us shouldn't drink at all but nevertheless do, and this creates another complex of problems. The tendencies, habits, symptoms, and behavior of both groups need study, research, and treatment, from each of a dozen points of view.

Meantime, the alcohol addict sits in the clinician's reception room. Who referred him? It may have been a police court, a judge, an institution for the mentally deranged, a welfare agency, a clergyman, a member of the family, a professor, an employer, a foreman, a union shop steward, a friend, the family doctor, the cop on the corner. And it is this multiplicity of possibilities that compels the clinician to familiarize himself with a dozen disciplines outside the expected scope of his specialty.

It is a large order, an engrossing one, and, fortunately, a rewarding one. It is also, if the therapist is to have any success in effecting recoveries among alcoholics, the routine and only order—at least, so far as is known at present. A psychiatrist, in treating a patient, treats him whole: the sum of his aspirations, confusions, bafflements, fears, guilts, and tensions; his dreams, his gestures, his habits, his expressions; his silences and his withdrawals; his moods and actions past, present, and projected; everything he thinks and feels and does: the whole individual. Comparably, the physician specializing in the treatment of alcoholism comes to realize that the sickness he is combating is a pathologic condition rooted in society, compounded out of its past and its present; conditioned by the family and the educational system; affected by all sorts of traditions, taboos, cultural considerations, social conformities, stimuli from advertising and from all the communication media; part and parcel of all the complexities and tensions of modern life. He discovers, moreover, that he may have to harness all of society's forces to treat one single individual.

We drink

I

In 1954 the American public bought and presumably drank 189,470,688 gallons of distilled spirits, 82,475,456 thirty-one-gallon barrels of malt beverages, and 176,204,279 gallons of wine. We can accept these figures because they comprise the basis on which the liquor industry—distillers, brewers, and vintners—is taxed by federal, state, and local governments.

It is a comfort to come on such a hard fact, specific, cognate, apparently incontrovertible. There is only one difficulty: it is not accurate. It does not tell us the whole truth about how much we drink in a year for it does not, as it cannot, take into account home-brew, homemade wine, or bootleg liquor. Any estimate of how much beer or hard cider is fermented at home for personal use would be the wildest sort of guesswork, and industry spokesmen agree with Treasury officials that it is inconsiderable, so we may ignore it. Those who wish to make wine for their own use are permitted to make up to two hundred gallons apiece without interference by the government; it may be presumed that most of those who do so are, typically, Italian-Americans; their total annual product does not tot up to much more than one million gallons and so may also be disregarded. Bootleg distilled spirits, moonshine, is something else again. Moonshine is big business.

Let us assume, however, that the figures cited tell the whole story. They are big numbers but by themselves they are relatively meaningless. We must poke them about a little before they will tell us anything.

We hope they have a great deal to tell us. Some part of those big numbers, we know, represented pathological drinking, alcoholism. Another considerable part, perhaps even more calamitous for society, meant excessive drinking, drunkenness. Somewhere, locked up in those big numbers, was a lot of erratic behavior—some of it pleasant, some of it silly, or evil, or thoughtless, or stupid, or cruel, or unintentionally homicidal —much of it totally foreign to our ordinary behavior. Somehow, too, those numbers represent a lot of hangovers, feelings of remorse and of guilt. We expect, before we are finished, to have fitted the numbers into relationship with the emotional behavior. We must come at them from various directions. Thus:

How many of us drink this much? How does this total work out per capita? Is it more than we drank a year ago? Fifteen years ago? A hundred years ago? What does it tell us about our drinking habits? Are we taking our alcohol today in different beverages than we did yesterday? How much do we spend on all this liquor? How big a chunk of our spending money does it represent?

And when we say *we* drink this much, whom are we talking about? Who are we? How old? Of which sex? Of which religious faith? From what ethnic background? How much does our religious or ethnic background influence our drinking habits? Or are they determined rather by the culture in which we presently live?

All those questions we must answer, but there is one that ranks the rest. It is this: Why do we drink alcoholic beverages? And in order to appreciate the discussion of that question, we must first establish what the chemical ethyl alcohol does to us when we drink it.

It is ethyl alcohol we are talking about when we speak of alcoholic beverages. About four-and-a-half per cent of beer is alcohol; ale is slightly stronger, maybe six or eight per cent alcohol; wines range from about twelve per cent to as much as twenty-three per cent alcohol, the stronger wines like port and sherry having been fortified; most distilled spirits are between forty and fifty per cent alcohol; some liqueurs, such as benedictine or absinthe, may be as much as sixty or sixty-five per cent alcohol. Absolute alcohol is two hundred proof; the phrase *ninety proof* on a bottle of spirits means that the contents are forty-five per cent alcohol. Traces of other alcoholic compounds can be found in any drink, but it is ethyl alcohol that produces the effect sought by the drinker. What is this alcohol?

Chemically, it is a compound: C_2H_5OH. Pharmacologically, it is not such a simple matter. For many years a misconception has ruled, that alcohol is a stimulant. Indeed, this myth still exerts a powerful grip. You can hear people claim that they work better, thanks to one, two, or three drinks; that alcohol inspires them to greater feats of muscle or more brilliant feats of mind. Demonstrably, neither can possibly be the case. Alcohol is no stimulant; it is a depressant. It seems to stimulate, especially if taken in a strong, straight gulp, which will cause a reflex, a gasp and a momentary increase in heart action. There is also the fact that alcohol in small amounts seems to give the feeling of elation, which in turn has led to the notion that it is a stimulant. But it is not. It is a depressant.

As to its further classification, we encounter, as usual, confusion and disagreement. In this corner, sits a physiologist of lofty reputation: he insists that alcohol is a volatile anaesthetic. In that corner sits a biochemist, equally eminent, who denies it is an anaesthetic and maintains it is a narcotic. The disagreement is, fortunately, not of great importance: alcohol has, all will agree, sedative effects when taken in small amounts; taken in rather larger doses its effect is narcotic; to some extent it combats pain and must therefore qualify also as an analgesic; and, drunk in sufficient quantity, it will operate as an anaesthetic and put the drinker to sleep.

In any event, it is a depressant.

And it is an intoxicant; which is to say, it is toxic, it is deleterious to the optimum functioning of the individual. Just as it is greatly toxic in large amounts, so it is mildly toxic in small amounts; but toxic it is in either event. To make such a judgment, one need not be a Dry, or a temperance advocate, or an abstainer, or overly endowed with a Puritan conscience. One need only know the swift effect of alcohol on the cells of the body.

When we take a drink, the alcohol in it is absorbed very rapidly into the blood. The speed of the process is affected by such factors as the kind of drink, whether it is diluted or not, and how much food there is in the stomach; in any event, however, the absorption of the alcohol into the blood is far quicker than that of almost anything else we eat or drink. It begins to be absorbed, indeed, even before it hits the stomach: inconsiderable amounts are taken into the blood through the mucous membrane of mouth, throat, and gullet. As much as two-fifths of the alcohol passes into the blood directly through the walls of the stomach; at first rapidly, and then rather more

15

slowly, it is absorbed by the network of capillaries around the stomach lining. The balance goes from the stomach into the small intestine where, as fast as it is received, it is also absorbed into the blood.

Since blood from in and around the digestive organs goes first, by way of the portal vein, to the liver, some small part of the alcohol is there oxidized. But not much: the liver cannot oxidize alcohol as fast as alcohol is absorbed into the blood. The greater part of the alcohol, then, mixes in the liver with blood from the lower part of the body, flows through the vena cava to the heart where it is further diluted by blood from the other parts of the body, and is then pumped by the heart throughout the circulatory system.

But—and this is crucial—the distribution of the alcohol through the body is not evenly balanced. It concentrates in some parts and shuns others. It makes its way to the cerebro-spinal fluid, it maintains a relatively high concentration in the blood, it is absorbed to a rather lesser extent in muscle tissue, it passes scarcely at all into bone and fat tissue. This has to do with the affinity of alcohol for water. It is quite as though nature is bent on diluting the alcohol if we have not, and diluting it further if we have. This may explain why it is absorbed so rapidly, and so unusually, into the blood through the walls of the stomach; for blood is about ninety per cent water. In any event, once in the circulatory system, the alcohol is distributed, to be diluted, to those parts of the body that have a high water content.

The cells of the brain are interlaced with blood vessels; they subsist in fluid. And so, after a very few minutes, the highest concentration of the alcohol is in the brain. Moreover, the first part of the brain affected by that alcohol is the cortex, precisely the area controlling the higher intellectual functions: behavior, speech, memory. Alcohol's direct impact is on the central nervous system; the disturbance is functional. The first impairment is to judgment. The second is to coordination. The third is to consciousness. The fourth, presuming that we carry our drinking that far, is to life.

But at the moment we are not concerned with such a dire toxicity. To be sure, if we drink hard and heavy over a long period of time, we may grossly disrupt a number of our physical functions; we may injure our liver, be overcome by any of several dietary deficiencies, inflame the throat or stomach, or otherwise prejudice our organic health. Such changes follow only on systematic excessive drinking. Just now we are interested only in so-called normal drinking, social drinking, the drinking, say, of two to five drinks in an evening. What does it do to us?

If before dinner you drink two dry martinis from a four-ounce glass, you will have swallowed about three ounces of absolute alcohol. If your weight is average—say 165 pounds— you will by the time you sit down to dinner have a concentration of about 0.14 per cent alcohol in your blood. This is sufficient to place you at the danger line, speaking from a medico-legal point of view. It is enough to dull your critical faculties, markedly impair your judgment, and loosen as well as thicken your tongue. Psychologists have arrayed a whole battery of tests designed to demonstrate how, at approximately this ratio of blood-alcohol, your perception, efficiency, ability to use memory, reaction to simple stimuli, performance of familiar and unfamiliar tasks, and discrimination of slight differences between intensities of light and sound are all impaired. (These tests fail to take account—as so shall we, for just a moment— of individual tolerance to alcohol and, more importantly, of mood and emotion, which obviously influence to a greater or lesser extent all such functions.)

The dinner you eat will now lower somewhat the concentration of alcohol in your blood, as will, with time, the process of oxidation. If, however, you should drink a couple of two-ounce whisky highballs after dinner, you would once again flunk the various psychological tests, and you would once again—depending on the speed with which you drank your highballs—be in danger of exceeding the medicolegal limit of 0.15 per cent. Intellectually, you would be your own inferior, no matter how much the contrary might seem to you to be the case.

The more you drink, the greater the validity of all these strictures.

But these strictures apply to the occasional social drinker. What about the heavy social drinker, the man (or woman) who habitually drinks anywhere from four to twelve or even more ounces of gin or whisky, or both, in an evening? Why is he apparently obedient to different physiological laws? What, in short, about the question of tolerance?

In the living room, in the night club, even on the highway, we have all of us been confronted with seemingly overwhelming evidence that there is such a phenomenon as greater tolerance to alcohol by some than by others. But it has not been so easy to demonstrate scientifically on a laboratory basis. Until recently this tempted us to conclude that such variations of behavior were to be attributed solely to psychological factors. A highly suggestible person, given a drink of flavored water which he has been told is a powerful intoxicant, will thereafter giggle, gab, prate, stagger, reel, stumble, and generally make quite a convincing fool of himself. Meantime, over in the corner sits a man who has smoothly and methodically packed away eight or ten ounces of whisky neat; he does not raise his voice, his behavior is sensible, and, when he chooses to go home, he does so with an even, purposeful gait. How come?

Moreover, one recovered alcoholic after another reports

that there were months or even years when he was able to drink impressive measures of alcohol, but that there came a time when his tolerance suddenly dropped to a point lower than had been the case even when he first started to drink. Presuming the observation to be accurate, is this organic or psychological?

Certainly habituation to the narcotic effects of alcohol leads to compensation. Perhaps unconsciously, the experienced drinker learns to steer clear of phrases that would trip his tongue, of actions that might betray the size of the load he is carrying. But habituation by itself cannot explain why this man will pass out when his blood-alcohol ratio reaches a given point while that man will not.

Physiologists, grappling with these questions, tried to answer them on the basis of a slower or less complete absorption of alcohol, but failed; on the basis of a more rapid excretion, but failed; on the basis of less penetration of alcohol into the brain, but failed; on the basis of swifter metabolism, but failed. They were left with the possibility that the brain of the more experienced drinker might be able to function despite the presence of alcohol either because of psychological factors or because of true tissue tolerance. But while psychological factors might govern the tolerance of a man with three or four drinks in him they could scarcely influence his behavior when his blood-alcohol ratio was in the neighborhood of 0.20 or 0.25 per cent. There remained the chance of true tissue tolerance.

To run laboratory tests on human subjects to establish the fact of such a matter might have raised eyebrows. But one may run such tests with animals. The thing was done: with dogs and rats. The convincing conclusion is that habituation to alcohol results in tolerance to the intoxicant. The central nervous system is capable of resisting the narcotic effects of

19

the drug. Dogs fed large doses of alcohol and habituated to them can walk around when the alcohol is concentrated in their blood at a level that would, before habituation, have felled them. Mercifully, these tests have not been carried to the point at which it can be clinically established that tolerance, after some time, falls again to a level lower than it was prior to habituation. Nor do such tests seem necessary. The results are in and satisfy the physiologists: brain cells can "learn" to get along with too much alcohol, at any rate for a time.

The question of tolerance to one side, there is, however, no doubt that drinking alcoholic beverages subverts, however fractionally, man's intellectual functions.

Confronted with only this side of the coin, it may seem puzzling why so many of us drink at all. Nor can it be contended that we who drink are so clouded in our judgment that we fail to realize how comparatively dull our drinking makes us. For every drinker has at some time had the experience of being sober among a group of acquaintances who have been drinking, and noticed how exhilarated they all were, how witty they all seemed to each other, how amused and amusing—but in reality how far they fell short of their self-conception, how inane they were, often how childish. Sometimes, in sheer self-defense, such a sober person drank "to catch up"—in reality, to slow down so that his opinion of the others might jibe with their self-conception.

Surely there must be another side of the coin. There must be powerful motives that compel us to drink when to do so, we know, means to toss overboard momentarily the best part of our greatest endowment. And indeed the motives are most powerful.

Let us call as the first witnesses to the nature and strength of these motives some of those of us who drink. True, their testimony may not be the best available; for the drinker may not know why he drinks or he may offer, instead of reasons, what are in fact merely socially acceptable rationalizations. Indeed, the drinker's reasons may undergo sea-changes with the years. Thus, for example, one woman of forty who has, during the ten years of her marriage, had at least two cocktails before dinner nearly every night, said swiftly in answer to the question as to why she drank: "To relax." Then she thought, and reconsidered, remembering how this habit had begun: "*Now* I drink to relax. But I started drinking to keep my husband company." She thought again—of her annual month-long holidays in the summer, when the days wheeled by without tension, and by preference she drank at the cocktail hour only a glass of white wine and seltzer—and added: "Sometimes I drink just to be sociable. To have a glass in my hand." Here are three perfectly valid expressions of motivation, one personal, one emulative, one social, all from the same person. And which of them, if any, contains the largest kernel of truth it would be hard to say.

Later on we shall have to call on other witnesses, scientists who are trained to interpret the patterns of drinking from the viewpoint of one or another discipline. But we can make a useful start by looking at the conscious attitudes of a respectably large sample of Americans who drink. They were elicited in 1946 by two sociologists * from 1,744 adult Americans.

The answers were divided into two general categories which seemed from the character of all the responses to be logical: individual reasons ("Makes me feel good," "I like it," "Because I'm thirsty," and so on) and social reasons ("To be sociable," "To keep my husband company," "At weddings or special occasions," and so on). These very broad groupings are apparently of about equal importance in inducing us to take

* John W. Riley, Jr. and Charles F. Marden, both of Rutgers University.

a drink: social reasons accounted for the drinking of 43 per cent of us, individual reasons for that of 41 per cent of us. The investigators were aware that such inclusive categories make quite strange bedfellows, as reflected in the individual responses. When a housewife says, "People think you're dead if you don't drink," her motive is qualitatively different from that of the man who says, "All of our friends drink, so we drink too"; yet both reasons are social. Comparably, a domestic employee answered, "A bottle of beer makes me feel rested after a hard day's work," and this is clearly an individual reason; but so is that of a salesman ("Why do I drink? To keep alive"), yet the latter answer could conceivably be pathological while the former can seem quite sensible.

This caveat having been entered, it is nevertheless possible to draw some instructive conclusions from an analysis of the survey. They have to do with the way motives change in relation to the drinker's sex, age, and frequency of drinking.

One half of the men, for example, drink for individual reasons, one third of them for social reasons; the reverse is true for the women. The younger one is, no matter of which sex, the more likely his drinking is to be attributed to social reasons; the older he is, the more likely he is drinking for individual reasons. The rates of change are steady. The same holds true when frequency of drinking is related to motivation. Three times as many daily drinkers are impelled by individual considerations as by social (59 per cent individual and 20 per cent social); of those that drink less than once a month, the reverse is true (23 per cent individual and 67 per cent social); and once again, the rates of change are steady through the various categories of drinking frequency.

To return for a moment to the woman of forty, married for ten years: she used not to drink more than once or twice a week and then for what were clearly social reasons ("I'd be asked out to dinner, maybe we'd go to a party"); she married and started to drink more often ("to keep my husband company"); she now drinks every evening ("to relax"), except during her annual summer vacation. In a sense, her changing habits reflect the changing patterns suggested by the survey. Frequency of drinking goes hand-in-hand with inner needs, and it appears that this crutch is used more often by the middle-aged than by the young.

But while one is young, emulation and social influences are the governing considerations. And this applies to teen-agers quite as much as to young adults, if not more so. So far we have been talking only about adults, just as though they were the only ones who drink; but of course this is not so. Some of us start drinking at twelve or thirteen. Those of us who grow up in families where wine is drunk as a matter of course with the meal may start even earlier. For fifteen-year-olds to drink with some regularity is by no means uncommon. The *why* of their drinking is more complex than for the adult, because there are, boiling within them, so many immiscible impulses. There is, in the first place, their attitude toward the law, which, while it changes as one crosses state lines, by and large forbids or attempts to curtail drinking by anyone less than eighteen years old. In the second place, there is the example of their parents and their parents' friends. But such an example may well throw them into direct conflict with the habits of their own friends: either to abstain or to drink. And surely at no age is the pressure of social conformity greater than when one is older than fourteen and younger than twenty-one. And, finally, the question of whether to drink or not to drink becomes a practical matter for many teen-agers at precisely the time when they are most forthrightly determined to challenge adult authority, to stay out later than a parent has permitted, to show an independence, to kick over a set of traces.

Habits of teen-agers have also come under the sociologists' lens. One study, of ten thousand high-school students, showed that one in three takes a drink at least occasionally. Another survey * indicated that drinking was even more widespread: eighty-six per cent of high-school youngsters on suburban Long Island drink at least occasionally. Three out of four of them reported that they were allowed to drink at home. Half of them were permitted, on occasion, to drink away from home. Those who were eighteen reported even more permissive sanctions: ninety-five per cent drink at home, eighty-four per cent away from home.

They were not asked why they drank. It is likely, however, that the teen-agers' motives are even more sensitively keyed to social pressures than is the case with the 21–25 age group studied as part of the survey of adults. In their case, fifty-one per cent drank for social reasons, thirty-six per cent for individual reasons. The rest drank either for both or for other reasons, or gave no reasons at all.

There is, furthermore, still a third study, by still another pair of sociologists,† that covers the overlapping age group of older teen-agers and younger adults. Investigated were the drinking habits and motivations of students in twenty-seven colleges and universities. Undergraduate drinkers were asked to grade a check list of thirteen reasons for drinking: which were of considerable importance in determining his (or her) use of alcohol, which were of some importance, and which of none. A conclusion was drawn from their answers: "It is apparent . . . that reasons having primarily a social connotation, e.g., 'to

*By two Hofstra College psychologists, Matthew N. Chappell and Herman Goldberg.
† Robert Straus and Selden D. Bacon. Their study, *Drinking in College*, published in 1953, was financed by the Yale Laboratory of Applied Physiology. Dr. Straus is at the State University Upstate Medical Center in Syracuse, N. Y.; Dr. Bacon is the director of the Yale Center of Alcohol Studies.

comply with custom,' 'to be gay,' 'to get along better on dates,' are generally considered of greater importance than those suggesting primarily a psychological motivation, e.g., 'as an aid in meeting crises,' 'to get drunk,' 'for a sense of well-being,' and 'in order not to be shy.' "

So we may add this evidence to that of the other surveys, and pause to reflect on it for a moment. It would seem, at least superficially, that our motives for drinking undergo a shift as we grow older. There is even a temptation to infer, as we look over the findings, that social pressures directly or indirectly lead a gradually increasing number of us into the habit of drinking with greater regularity, and that our habit of drinking becomes inevitably more necessary to us—why? Because we like it? Because it tastes good? Because we want to be gay? Because we want to relax? Because it makes us feel good? Because everybody else is doing it? To be sociable?

But such reasons are nonsense when juxtaposed with the narcotic effects of the drug. Surely these cannot be the powerful motives which, it was posited, must exist, to induce us to cramp our judgment and unfit, even if only temporarily, our best ability to function.

No, no; we have to thank these witnesses, the drinkers, for their testimony, but it is not enough. With the best of intentions, they have nevertheless told us very little about the why of our drinking, save for something negative: that most of us do not fully understand why we drink. They have been honest witnesses, but clearly honesty is not a sharp enough tool to get at the truth.

We need more competent witnesses. We can summon first the social scientists, students of our societal behavior.* They are interested in the extent to which a society, by its complex-

* Of whom one of the most thoughtful and experienced in the problems of alcohol and alcoholism is Selden Bacon of Yale. We draw, at this point, on some of Dr. Bacon's ideas, but decline to burden him with our conclusions.

ity, sets up tensions in its members. They are interested in the society's attitudes and sanctions influencing the drinking of its members. And, but by no means finally, they are interested in whether suitable substitutes for drinking can be found.

The social scientists attempt to see modern American society whole; certainly they see it enormously snarled by complexities. Some of the threads in this tangle they have labeled with tags reading Stratification, or Specialization, or Competition. One of their primary concerns is the interaction of social groups; they note where such groups clash and why, and try objectively to assess the power of groups to endure and live at peace with each other for their mutual benefit and their social progress. And in this process, the social scientists perceive an important role played by alcohol.

They have observed that, in contrast to older, simpler, earlier societies, ours is beset by group antagonisms and conflicts, interest against interest: the boss against the union, one political party against another, one church group against another, the aged left out in the cold, women the object of a special discrimination, religious or ethnic minorities reviled, and so on. They note, further, that the job specialization which is the natural end result of modern production techniques has led to increasing ignorance on the part of each of us about all the rest of us. And where there is ignorance, there is fertile soil for suspicion and mistrust and hostility.

They perceive that the strongest bond holding our contrary groups together is recreation. Here is our chief common ground. And here, chiefly, is why the consumption of recreation has become so important in our frighteningly complex society. We consume recreation in great gobs: television, the movies, radio, professional and amateur sports, card games, gambling of all kinds. And, as like as not, we wash the gobs down with alcoholic beverages. Consider how important an adjunct to the country club is the nineteenth hole; consider how remunerative a business is the catering at professional baseball games or at race tracks; consider the cocktail party; consider how routine is the serving of alcoholic beverages to friends who drop in of an evening to watch television. The two are associated: alcohol and recreation. Alcohol is the solvent that enables the wheels of our recreational life to turn smoothly.*

To the sociologist, with his vision of our whole society, such solvents are critically important. Without them, the antagonisms engendered by the society might well explode.

His vision can be reduced to caricature, but the caricature may be helpful. To him, an individual is representative of our tremulously balanced social groupings. Call a man a white Episcopalian male Republican employer, of Anglo-Dutch ethnic stock, and you have assigned him in one breath to six subgroups and by no means exhausted the possibilities, only the obvious ones. For may he not also be a Wet? a golf-player? an anti-vivisectionist? a college man? He is in any event stratified: his tendency will be to associate by preference only with other white male Episcopalian Republican employers who are of Anglo-Dutch stock. If, in addition, his associates are golf-playing anti-vivisectionist college men, so much the better from his point of view.

But the sociologist is not so sure. The sociologist wonders whether, for the health of society, it would not be salutary to break down the many-layered walls of such a man's compartment. The sociologist sees society fractionalized. He would like to see such a compartmentalized man mix freely and easily

* In Britain, owners of public houses have been asked not to install television sets in areas where home influences are weak (notably the seaports) lest young people be exposed to protracted sessions of viewing and drinking. The request was made in a report which it was found necessary to make on "television and drunkenness."

with, say, a Catholic Democratic trade-union official of Slavic ethnic stock, or an agnostic college professor of mixed ethnic stock, or a Baptist Negro woman who works as a domestic employee.

There is, the sociologist acknowledges, precious little chance that such a quartet could ever become bosom friends. The chance of their ever coming together under one roof, in our society, is slim; perhaps the only chance would be if they all attended the same recreational event, perhaps a movie.

Where else could they meet? In the home of none of them, for reasons of choice or prejudice; not in a restaurant around the same table, for the same reasons; not in church; not on the golf links; not at an alumni reunion; not at the meeting of a trade association, or a union meeting, or a Rotary Club luncheon. If by some wild chance all were baseball fans, still one would sit in a box, another in the grandstand, another in the upper tier, and the fourth in the bleachers. Put them all together in one room and the air would be electric with suspicion, snobbery, and hostility, each for the other. Conversation would die a-borning. Communication, always a delicate flower, would wither on its stalk.

But give each of them two or three or four drinks, and see what would happen.

Perhaps such a caricature example is too extreme. Return, then, to the white male Episcopalian Republican employer, of Anglo-Dutch stock. Invite him to a gathering of three or thirty others, every one like him in every particular save one. Make all the others Negroes, or women, or Catholics, or Democrats, or hired workers, or of Italian stock, but otherwise like him in every other particular. Still, we will recognize, he will be prey—and so will the others—to embarrassment, to suspicion and hostility.

Until and unless all hands have downed a drink or two.

And so the sociologist sees a function for alcohol in our society, and a logical motive for our drinking it.* The individual who, in his infinite variety, makes up society is not *per se* the sociologist's cup of tea; but still, observing how hostility is charged up in him by the complex stratification and specialization of modern life—and most of all by its competition—the sociologist comes to understand the individual's why of drinking. He sees the one man or woman eaten by doubts and anxieties: about his prestige, about his job, about his security, about sex, about his weekly wage, about his executive responsibilities and how to remain calm in the face of them, about himself and what he thinks of himself and what he thinks his friends think of him. The sociologist sees alcohol fulfilling an obligatory role for this individual in each of his different guises. He recognizes that alcohol often offers a welcome escape from the tensions and anxieties of the snarl of life.

This would, however, avail the individual nothing if society refused him alcohol. So the sociologist, inquiring further, determines what, in our particular society, are the several discrete attitudes toward alcohol that color our individual approaches to it. They can be, each of them, defined and typified. They are: the abstinent, the ritual, the dietary, the convivial, and the utilitarian or functional.

* So does the United States government. Annually, the State Department asks the Congress for funds so that diplomats overseas may wine and dine foreign officials. In fiscal 1954-55 this sum was $475,000; Deputy Under Secretary of State Loy Henderson asked for an increase to $700,000 for fiscal 1955-56. "If we are to perform our work properly," said Henderson, "we have to have these pleasant social relations not only with the representatives of the local government but with other leaders of the community and also with fellow diplomats representing countries with which it is important we maintain friendly relations. This is part of the work of our service. . . . United States interests have suffered because of [our diplomats'] inability to form and maintain the necessary contacts." The appropriation has been nicknamed the "whisky allowance" by Congressmen.

Abstinence requires, to be totally effective, a society which is emotionally monochrome and ideologically monolithic. Since it is doubtful that a society will ever come into being that satisfies both these requirements, it may be doubted that abstinence can ever become an effective viewpoint for the totality. Certainly it was not effective in the United States; nor does it work where, as in Islam, it is a religious doctrine. An abstinent social unit, like a family, discovers irrevocably that its young are variously minded about such a sanction: they may be rebellious, they may be submissive, they may go through torments as they waver between these two poles, they may fall victim to overwhelming if momentary emotional moods and storms. At the same time, it should be noted that, for one reason or another, abstinence is the choice of about one-third of the physically mature population of the United States. It is not within our present province to inquire as to why the abstainers choose to abstain. But surely no one will argue that they are not also prey to tensions and conflicts imposed on them both from within themselves and from without. The fact that they have succeeded in finding other ways of releasing their tensions and escaping their anxieties (tea, coffee, music, dancing, whatever) is at least proof that alcohol is not the only solution.

Ritual drinking is more than permissive; it is exacted. To be sure, it is also, usually, temperate. It is bound up with religious ceremony, of which it is a part; in our society it motivates many professing Christians and all religious Jews.

Dietary drinking is akin to ritual drinking in that it is temperate and occasional. Here the occasion is the meal time. Formerly it motivated those of us who are first- or second-generation Americans, and especially those of us from the Mediterranean basin; such of us drank only with our meals, and then usually wine. The spread of the habit is slow but steady. But at the same time, another change is being worked:

some of those who used to drink only wine are conforming to the socially more customary American drinking of spirits instead.

Convivial drinking, drinking for jollification, is also akin to ritual drinking, save that here the ritual is social rather than religious. This, by and large, accounts for all the drinking which the drinkers themselves describe as social—and probably a good deal of what they describe as individual as well. Here is the drinking that aims at the creation of social solidarity, the drinking that breaks down the compartments walling us one from another; the drinking of the stag party, the locker room, the corner saloon; the festive drinking that leads to the singing of "Sweet Adeline"; where all are good fellows together, and the dams break and joviality is the aim but not, strictly speaking, always the end result.

Utilitarian drinking, functional drinking, is likely to go on in either of two places: as an accompaniment to a business transaction, or individualistically, at home, alone or in company with one or two others. Both types are of great importance in the American culture. Business drinking is a relatively latter-day phenomenon. F. Scott Fitzgerald, in one of his autobiographical essays, remarks that in 1920 he "shocked a rising young businessman by suggesting a cocktail before lunch." Today, in some business circles, the shock would be felt only if the cocktail were not routinely ordered. It serves, again, an important function, one of which the sociologist is keenly aware: it breaks the ice, it enables the deal to be made, the contract to be signed, the sale to be consummated. And later, at home, in the evening, when the individual withdraws to contemplate himself, he drinks again, in quite utilitarian fashion, to make peace with himself.

And why not? Here are, for the sociologist's satisfaction, four motives that impel us to drink alcoholic beverages. What substance is there, calculated to function better or as well in the achievement of these socially desirable ends?

Some of us narcotize ourselves with other drugs, to be sure: marijuana (which is hemp, or hashish), various morphine derivatives, cocaine—but these are all socially reprehensible in the United States (though not in some foreign countries). Some of us sniff ether, to go on a jag, to summon euphoria; and the chemical similarity, ether to ethyl alcohol, is suggestive—ether is $(C_2H_5)_2O$; ethyl alcohol is C_2H_5OH—while the effects are even more similar; but ether is highly volatile, dangerously so.

Viewed pragmatically, there is no intoxicating drug so satisfactory for human consumption as ethyl alcohol. Its effects, if it is not taken in too large doses, are reversible; it mixes easily with water; it can be cunningly and pleasurably disguised so that its taste is by no means objectionable; its boiling point is higher than body temperature, which means that it will not develop a high vapor pressure in the stomach after it has been swallowed.

So, to sum up the sociological view of why we drink: we are all of us charged with tensions ascribable to the society in which we have our being; this society encourages us to drink alcoholic beverages in order to quell our tensions and get along better with each other; alcohol is the best available substance with which to do the job.

This view cannot be faulted, except in one niggling respect. The sociologist examines the question of why "we" drink, and to him "we" is a social group and "drinking" a social function. It is not his province to probe any further beneath the conscious surface, nor is it his interest. But it must be ours.

We want to know why we as individuals seek to narcotize ourselves, why you and you and you and I have the impulse to swallow with varying regularity a toxic agent. There are conscious reasons, but they do not persuade. There are social reasons, but they are not enough. There must be also very strong unconscious psychic reasons. We should, if we are to recognize the necessities that lie behind our drinking, understand as much as possible about these psychic reasons, and thereby free ourselves from any emotional commitment to accept or refuse a drink. We should, in brief, know why we do what we do. And so we must summon the psychoanalyst.

There may be a few who will object that the psychoanalyst has no business here: that his concern is with neuroses, with neurotic behavior, with the sick, if it is anywhere; and that there is nothing pathological about a man taking a drink if he wants to.

While we may agree there is nothing unhealthy about taking a drink, the other half of the objection must be ruled out. The psychoanalyst is concerned with more than the neurotic, he is concerned with the unconscious. To be sure, therapeutically the psychoanalyst undertakes to assist his patients in combating their neuroses. But in terms of his field of theoretical medicine, he addresses himself to the understanding of mental life, in which the unconscious demonstrably plays a crucial role.

Moreover, while there are patent differences between social drinking and alcohol addiction, no one will deny that there are also similarities. If we know the unconscious motives that recommend the one, it will be of great help in establishing the etiology of the other.

At this point the voice of the skeptic can be heard, denying that his reasons for taking a drink are unconscious, vehemently insisting that they are conscious, manifest, and controlled. We solicit his skepticism. Freud remarked that a benevolent skepticism toward the scientific method of psychoanalysis should be encouraged. Nor is there any disposition to deny the importance of the drinker's conscious act of volition, his manifest wish to have a drink. What is argued is that the reason he arrives at the conscious wish, the timing of the wish, the context and content of the wish, are all colored by impulses originating in his unconscious.

The most skeptical, for his part, can scarcely deny the existence of an unconscious and the impact of its demands on us all. Every day of our lives is crammed with impulses, thoughts, emotions, lapses of tongue or memory, all of which could be traced, if there were need or patience to do so, back to the unconscious. It is, so to say, an echo chamber storing up the stimuli we once received and to which we once reacted and, in appropriate situations, when triggered, making its presence felt in appropriately reactive fashion.

The unconscious is a world of instinctual activity. It must be urged that by *instinctual* is not intended something fixed and immutable, innate and inherited, but rather a complex adaptive state of tension demanding discharge. Arguments still rage over the proper definition and classification of instincts, but this debate need not detain us; we are interested not in speculation but in the empirical experience of the instinctual impulses and in how these impulses arise.

It is generally agreed that the sexual instincts, on their way to healthy maturity, go through several changes. They are first manifest in infancy, during which the ego is in process of being differentiated and developed by means of specific stages of libidinal organization.* Of these stages, the first is called oral-erotic and extends, speaking generally, over the first twelve to fifteen months of life; the second, which appears during the second year of life, is called anal-sadistic; the third, which marks the end of infancy, is called the genital. These names were not capriciously arrived at, but were deliberately se-

---

* Libido was defined by Freud as the motor force of sexual life and characterized as "a quantitative energy directed to an object."

lected * as best describing, on the basis of observation, the infant's libidinal impulses during the course of growth. And the stages they describe are of concern to the present discussion for the reason that, in every one of us, to a greater or lesser extent, there remain vestiges of each stage which appear as governing impulses, as echoes or reflections, from the unconscious.

If emotional growth is grossly retarded at any point, the individual is said to be fixated at that point. The nature, intensity, and locus of his fixation are assessed by the psychoanalyst in order that he may diagnose the kind of neurosis and thereafter treat it.

If emotional growth is not retarded but develops in healthy fashion, the pre-adult sexual instincts will, after the infantile period, be for a time latent, after which they reappear with the onset of puberty. Subsequently, it may be presumed, the sexual instincts will arrive at the final genital stage, and the individual will be prepared to love a person of the opposite sex quite normally. But that individual will, no matter how successful the process of his mental and emotional maturation, retain traces in his unconscious of all the stages through which he has passed.

Of these stages, the one pertinent at the moment is the oral-erotic. (It might, more accurately, be referred to as the intestinal-erotic, as describing the infantile pleasure that results from a stomach filled with warm food; but there are persuasive reasons for thinking of the mouth and lips as the decisive erotogenic area for the very young infant.) Throughout the first year of life, but especially in its earlier days, the infant has a regular rhythm: hunger and sleep—or, to put it in another

* By Freud. Other analytic schools use differing phrases. Thus, for example, Dr. William V. Silverberg describes the first period as that characterized by problems of orality and deprivation; the second as that characterized by problems of discipline; the third as that characterized by problems of rivalry and genitality.

way, tension and relaxation. Hunger goads him awake and into tension and, in the words of Gesell,* at four weeks "He awakes with a decisive, piercing cry." There is only one thing that can relieve his tension: satiety. With satiety, he falls asleep again. At sixteen weeks, "He may wake with a prompt cry to announce that he is hungry." Now he knows what will relieve his tension: "Hands may come to the breast or may grasp at clothes as the infant secures the nipple with very little assistance from the adult. . . . Lips are pursed at the corners and sucking is strong . . . . After initial satiety the infant may release and re-secure the breast repeatedly in a playful manner, with smiling." Reality is, at this point for the infant, an object that he longs for (the breast) in order to achieve the gratification of an even more powerful longing (relaxation of tension: sleep). At twenty-eight weeks, "He differentiates between people, and demands more of the one who feeds him," since she is still necessary to the relaxation of the tension within him. At this age, he may no longer suck his thumb or fingers before and after feedings; now instead he may bring "objects to his mouth and chew them." At forty weeks, he enjoys lip play "which consists of patting his lips to induce singing." From all these signs, we can deduce that his oral mucous membrane is erogenous; he derives pleasure from its stimulation, pleasure quite distinct from the satisfaction of his hunger.

The pleasure has a clear objective: to relieve tension.

The pleasure has an object by which its objective is attained: the mother's breast, or the nipple of the bottle.

The pleasure is instinctual.

Now, there are several possibilities that may take place in the life of the slowly differentiating ego of the infant during

* Dr. Arnold Gesell, Director of the Clinic of Child Development, School of Medicine, Yale University. The quotations are from *Infant and Child in the Culture of Today* by Dr. Gesell and Dr. Frances L. Ilg, in collaboration with others.

this period, but let us suppose that there are only two: on the one hand, the infant regards this stage in his development as so pleasurable that he forever after regrets having to take leave of it and forever after would like to return to it; and, on the other hand, the infant feels deprived, feels that in some way he has not been granted all the satiety which was his due, and in consequence feels forever after that he would like to return to it in order to get that of which he feels he was deprived.

As can be imagined, the differences in degree between these two polar possibilities are enormous. Somewhere between them there must be an ideal and theoretical mean: an infant thoroughly satisfied with what he has received and eager to see what the future holds for him. Just as obviously there must be, between the theoretical mean and the two poles, the great bulk of us—men and women who bear, in our unconscious echo chambers, memory-traces of tension unrelaxed, or of tension so deliciously discharged that if only we could have the same now, how wonderful the world would be! That tension, we remember, that awful, intolerable, scream-provoking, miserable, dangerous, depressing tension, was relieved by an object that we were able to suck: "Some cry vigorously . . . as the mother exposes her breast, in anticipation."

And so, oppressed however faintly by the imminent approach of some other realistically unrelated danger, depression, misery, tension, even trivial nuisance, we react impulsively. We seek to meet the threat by recourse to a pleasurable stimulation of the oral mucous membrane, which we remember from infancy as being erogenous.

We kiss. We smoke. We take a drink.

We take a drink. And the alcohol achieves for us the same happy result achieved, long years before, by the milk of our mothers.

But the alcohol does something else, something pharmacological, that bears a striking similarity to another infantile need.

In the early part of the oral-erotic stage, before the baby has so much as defined the object (the breast) which relieves his tension, he is almost entirely autoerotic. His sexual instincts are wholly narcissistic. He feels himself omnipotent, and delights in the feeling. By omnipotence we do not mean a divine power over every conceivable thing in the universe, but we do mean a power over everything the baby can conceive of in *his* small and circumscribed universe. When he cries, presto! something happens to answer and relieve. Nothing is better calculated to maintain the baby's self-esteem at a high level. The only thing that threatens the height of his self-esteem is his regularly recurring hunger. And so he is exacting in his demands, for what is more pleasurable than the feeling of being all-powerful? To refer again to Gesell, the baby at sixteen weeks "expects certain things to happen," he cries "if his patience spell is imposed upon," for to him relief of tension and a resumption of the sense of omnipotence are the same thing.

And what does alcohol do? Even on the conscious level, we may remind ourselves, drinkers gave answers like "It makes me feel good" and "To be gay" and "For a sense of well-being" and "In order not to be shy"—in short, to heighten self-esteem.

To heighten our self-esteem, we must temporarily paralyze our superego, which performs the disagreeable function of transforming our instinctual pleasure impulses into feelings of guilt, of suppressing some of our pleasure-drives, of diminishing our self-esteem. On this score, it is pertinent to note that someone has defined the superego as "that part of the mind that is soluble in alcohol." What stronger motivation could most of us have for an occasional drink? or, indeed, for an habitual drink?

The wonder no longer is that any of us drink. The wonder is rather that all of us do not drink, and more, and more often.

If the individual's emotional growth were wholly bound up in what occurs during the first year or so of life, it is likely that we all would. Quite obviously this is not the case. The ego continues its painful march along the chastening path of reality. We come to understand that self-esteem is more properly based on one's own achievements, and that these in turn are accomplished in a social environment, a world not of objects but of people whose rights and dignity must be respected. Along the line this process of acculturation teaches us that we must live according to the dictates of various internal and external forces: God, our parents, the law, our conscience, the superego.

But deep within us always stir the ancient desires.

II

To heighten our self-esteem, to abolish tension and anxiety, to dispel the threat of danger, to serve the search for pleasure, to banish the self-recriminations of guilt. They are indeed very ancient desires: ancient in the history of the individual, ancient in the history of the race. The specific form of danger has changed, the choice of specific pleasure has varied over the course of the centuries, but the instinctual strivings have stayed the same.

Alcohol, as a servant of those desires, is only a little less ancient. The archaeologists are satisfied that potable alcohol was discovered at about the time when man relinquished his nomadic life and took up agriculture. Some anthropologists incline to the belief that naturally fermented wines antedate even agriculture. It would not have been, in any event, a very difficult discovery; it required of man no particular ingenuity. It could even, if you like to think of it that way, have come about through man's carelessness and stupidity, for nature will make wine from berries left negligently in some primitive bit of pottery or container of bark. And if one man were so stupid that he could not put together cause and effect, no matter; for another would have been able to; in fact, many others did. For it can be demonstrated that alcoholic beverages have been fermented and brewed all over the world, on each of the continental land-spaces, without regard to communication between them, from time immemorial.

Truly, having discovered that he feared, man was prompt to find a way to dispel his fear, at least for a brief time.

The number of primitive tribes that did not avail themselves of what nature was prepared to brew for them is notable because it is so small. A handful of nomadic hunters and gatherers of seeds: the Eskimos, in fact most of the peoples of the Arctic regions; the Australian bushmen; the Indians of northern and western North America and of the southernmost part of South America; some of the islanders of the Pacific, where, however, there was often some sort of substitute. Every other tribe and people of whom we have any knowledge had either discovered the process or learned it by example of a neighbor.

All kinds of things were brewed—anything that nature had supplied with sugar: fruits, berries, saps of cactus and palm, juice of sugar cane, milk of mare and cow and goat, root of beet and cassava, grains in their endless profusion. In Asia, rice wine; in North and Central America, beer from maize; in South America, beer from the cassava; around the Mediterranean basin, wine from date and grape; in Africa, beer from millet or mead from honey.

Knowing now something of the effects of even a little alcohol on the relatively civilized man, we may dare to conclude that, for the savage, the discovery was devastating, even cataclysmic.

Such an idea is supported by the anthropologist. He is privileged, from his observation of present-day primitive social groups, to draw an inference as to the behavior of all primitive societies when confronted with alcoholic beverages.

What does the primitive, or semi-primitive, native do when he gets his hands on alcohol?

He drinks, with no regard whatsoever for temperance or moderation. He drinks until he is drunk, until he is stupefied. Waking, he drinks again, until he has nothing left to drink.

It is—perhaps sobering is not quite the right word—chilling to reflect on the explosive combination of primitive man, uninhibited, for whom to think is to act, and alcohol. We are at the moment not thinking of the contemporary primitive, on whom civilization may already have imposed some restraints, but of the savage who stands in the dawn of man's era on earth.

The anthropologist can tell us something more of this early savage's attitudes toward alcohol, reasoning from the example of today's primitives. He can tell us, for example, that savage tribes do not, each one of them, react in the same way to the drug. Their drinking increases in proportion to their anxiety, we are told; and this seems a most reasonable inference. There are some semi-primitive tribes today, blessed with a relatively easy-going climate, a fertile soil, and an equable temperament; for these fortunates millet-beer is abundant and so is food; they drink a lot, but it is reported that their drunkenness results only in laughter, fun and games, and at length sleep. (But still they need to drink.) Such societies, as might be expected in this bad old world, are the exceptions. The anthropologist is at pains to remind us of all the anxieties that more typically harass primitive societies: their physical environment, of which they have little knowledge and over which they have less control; disease, often epidemic; the constant threat of forays by their neighbors, some of whom indeed may be head-hunters; the constant fear of crop-failure; and so on. All of those cited, it will be noted, are exogenous anxieties; that is to say, they are environmental, from outside the individual.

We suggest that these anxieties were, as well, endogenous, that is, springing from emotional conflicts within the individual. We postulate a monstrous guilt harbored by primitive man and closely associated with his use of alcohol. Although we recognize that the theory is entirely suppositious, there is, we believe, evidence in abundance to back it up.

In *Totem and Taboo*, Freud hypothesized the origin of the Oedipus complex in a long-gone day when men moved in hordes, led by a chief, "a violent, jealous father" who kept all the females for himself and drove away the growing sons. "One day the expelled brothers joined forces, slew and ate the father, and thus put an end to the father horde. Together they dared and accomplished what would have remained impossible for them singly. *Perhaps some advance in culture, like the use of a new weapon, had given them the feeling of superiority.* [This emphasis is ours.] Of course these cannibalistic savages ate their victim. This violent primal father had surely been the envied and feared model for each of the brothers. Now they accomplished their identification with him by devouring him and each acquired a part of his strength. The totem feast, which is perhaps mankind's first celebration, would be the repetition and commemoration of this memorable criminal act with which so many things began, social organization, moral restrictions, and religion."

This was the primal sin, and it was part of Freud's hypothesis that the parricide transformed the father horde into the brother clan, sanctified by common blood and emphasizing solidarity. "Society is now based on complicity in the common crime, religion on the sense of guilt and the consequent remorse, while morality is based partly on the necessities of society and partly on the expiation which this sense of guilt demands."

It is not necessary for us to recapitulate Freud's arguments, and we must resist the temptation to offer material (which is in any event familiar to cultural and social anthropologists and students of folklore) showing the significance among ancient peoples of the totem and totemic ritual. We will merely suggest that the "advance in culture" which, Freud noted, would have "given them the feeling of superiority" and nerved the sons to their bloody deed might well have been alcohol.

If this theory is correct, then it would follow that alcohol would have been of great importance in the totem feasts of ancient times and in the later developing religious forms.

So it was and is.

Further, it would follow that elaborate myths would have to be invented in order to conceal and forget the deed.

So they were. Like dreams, myths are often compounded of symbols; like dreams, they contain a kernel of truth; like dreams, they employ all sorts of substitute formations and distortion devices. And, as Freud pointed out, "A process like the removal of the primal father by the band of brothers must have left ineradicable traces in the history of mankind and must have expressed itself the more frequently in numerous substitutive formations the less it itself was to be remembered." Clearly there were important reasons for mankind's attempting to forget the terrible deed.

One such myth is that of Dionysus. Zeus, in the guise of a serpent, lay with Persephone, and she bore him Zagreus, or Dionysus. As a newborn baby, Dionysus aped his father, climbing to his throne and brandishing the lightning which was his father's emblem of authority. His triumphant escapade was brief: the Titans fell on him and, despite his frantic attempts to escape by metamorphosing himself into various symbolic figures, slashed him to bits. But he was reborn, and his sacred rites celebrate his resurrection.

Aside from the obvious parallel of his violent death and that of the primal father, what is there to suggest that this myth draws a symbolic cloak over an actual primordial crime? There is, first, the fact that the mother of Dionysus was Persephone, the Corn-Maiden, the goddess who annually, at spring-time, ascends from the underworld, the embodiment of fruitful grain. Her totemic significance is obvious. Again, the murdered Dionysus was, when attacked, playing the part of Zeus, the Father; indeed, one of the forms he assumed to escape the Titans *was* that of Zeus (it was as a bull that he was killed). And again, the Titans were, according to myth, the ancestors of men; we are all descended from these murderers.

Moreover, the myth of Dionysus was of great importance in the ancient world. His death and resurrection are the core of the Eleusinian mysteries, a religion of considerable significance in Greece and indeed throughout the eastern end of the Mediterranean basin. Nor is his myth without parallels. His story and the ceremonial rite of his religion have so many points of similarity with those of the Egyptian god Osiris that it has been supposed the Greeks stole the religion entire from Egypt. But the similarity is to be explained on quite different grounds: the myths of the two gods sprang from similar folk-experience: Dionysus is definitely Thracian in origin. There are, additionally, points of correspondence between Dionysus and Mithras, from the Persian pantheon; and indeed with other ancient gods from quite different parts of the world.

But if our theory is to be justified, we would suppose that in such a myth a prominent feature would be alcohol.

And so it is. Dionysus (whom we know also as Bacchus) is the god of the vine, the god of the grape, the god of wine.

When first these gods were created by man they were not anthropomorphic, they were animistic. They were the thing itself. The god was no man-shaped figure wearing symbolic vine-leaves woven into a crown; he was the vine itself. And, as Frazer * reminds us, "The juice of the grape is his blood. . . . Thus the drinking of wine in the rites of a vine-god like Dionysus is not an act of revelry, it is a solemn sacrament." "When we call corn Ceres and wine Bacchus," wrote Cicero, "we use a common figure of speech; but do you imagine that anybody is so insane as to believe that the thing he feeds upon is a god?" But in fact that was precisely what Cicero's ancestors did believe.

Finally, if our theory is correct, we would suppose that throughout the pre-history and history of man, his attitude toward alcohol would be compounded of intensely ambivalent, conflicting emotions.

So it has always been, and so it is.

This is why the Eleusinian mysteries were such a compelling religion. The sons had ambivalent feelings for the father they slew: they hated him, but they loved him; and so in the Dionysian rites their descendants celebrate his death, but contrive to make him immortal. And what is slain is no longer the primal father; that part of the deed is cloaked by mythic distortion; it is now the vine that is killed. It is as though the sons are saying: "We didn't do it, we are not the guilty ones, we are not to blame! It is the wine we drank! The wine is guilty of the murder!" Just so a child will say: "*I* didn't do it, my hand did."

It is, when we think of it, difficult to conceive of a human discovery, an artifact, around which have whirled such sharply conflicting emotions. Consider, on the one hand, how it has as

* Sir James G. Frazer, whose *The Golden Bough* is a monumental study in magic and religion.

a custom survived and triumphed over the competition of other, comparable customs; that is to say, how utterly it seems to fulfill a need. Weapons have changed, transport has changed, clothing has changed, modes of shelter have changed—but alcoholic beverages, very little changed, are with us still. Consider, on the other hand, how we have in every age—one is tempted to say in every day of every week of every year of every age—fought to control this custom, if not to prohibit it outright; that is to say, how dangerous, how sinful we have conceived it to be. But our efforts have been unavailing.

At once we must have it but are fearful of it; drink it but deny it; love it and hate it; try to kill it but keep it immortal. Here indeed is a magical substance.*

Significantly, the earliest † efforts to restrain the use of alcohol seem to have been addressed precisely toward the avoidance of any repetition of the primal sin. Women—the incestuous cause of the original conflict—are prohibited from joining in the communal drinking even though they may well have been the brewers or wine-makers. The young men are likewise barred: they are, after all, sons of living fathers and must at all costs be forbidden the explosive opportunity of emulating their ancestors. (In at least one semi-primitive society, the Elgeyo of Kenya, it is reported this taboo is carried to such lengths that, except on ceremonial occasions, only the elders of the tribe are permitted to drink.) As like as not, weapons are taken from those who are about to drink.

Other reasons can, of course, be postulated for the existence of each of these restrictions, and there is no disposition on our part to deny the cogency of such reasons. Men may fight over

---

* The Greek word φάρμακον means "drug"; it means also "poison"; and among the ancient Greeks it meant, as well, "magical substance"; a very pretty philological expression of our ambivalence.
† Judging from the restrictive practices of current primitive societies.

women; younger men, perhaps because of their lesser experience, may be more swiftly inclined to wrath; weapons and alcohol may not mix under the best of circumstances. The pragmatic test of experience could have led in each case to such restrictions. And there are surely hostilities, anxieties, and guilts that do not stem from any primordial crime. But having agreed to all this, we are still confronted by the phenomenon of a continuing intensity of ambivalent emotional attitudes toward beverage alcohol—an intensity out of all proportion to the reality of the ordinary effects of the drug. We believe it can be understood only in the light of our hypothesis.

It is in this light, too, that we can interpret the severity of the repressive methods attempted against the alcohol traffic. Records of these efforts stud our written history. One of the earliest extant legal codes, that of Hammurabi, king of Babylonia two thousand years before the Christian era, includes, to be sure, relatively mild regulations. But in China at about the same time it is recorded that a vintner was banished for making wine; much later the government was attempting to control intoxicants by monopolizing manufacture and sale; in the fifth century A.D. an imperial edict proclaimed that all liquor makers, sellers, or users were to have their heads chopped off; in the thirteenth century Kublai Khan announced sentence of banishment and slavery for all engaged in the liquor traffic. In Egypt there was a period when the priests forbade the use of intoxicants. The Hindus also at one time made the manufacture, transportation, sale, barter, or use of liquor a capital offense. This would seem to have covered every base, but it was unavailing. The apothegms of the Hebrews reflect, again, the ambivalence: "Drink not and you will not sin," it is written in the Talmud, and also, "Wine ends in blood," but it is also written, "There is no gladness without wine." Among the Greeks, Plato urged that wine be forbidden all those under

47

thirty years of age. The Roman law took note that crimes might be committed under the influence of alcohol taken specifically for the purpose, and dealt with them more sternly than those committed while the miscreant was sober.

With the onset of the Christian era, St. Paul urged now moderation, now abstinence. The handful of desert monastic sects practiced an ascetic abstinence, the Church demanded penance of the habitual drunkard, and there were as time went on frequent *ex cathedra* denunciations of drunkenness, but drinking continued to be a widespread habit. At first, of course, the Church had no legal arm with which to enforce its pleas, but the later Roman emperors were as concerned as the early Christian leaders: Domitian, for example, decreed that half the Italian vineyards be destroyed. But still the people drank.

The founding of Mohammedanism in the early 600's brought about an important change of attitude toward liquor, for what was to become a significant slice of humanity. The prophet himself forbade his followers the use of any alcoholic beverages. He demanded total abstinence. There are some cynics who hold that he arrived at this decision out of a recognition that any new religion, if it is to have a chance of success, must be predicated on novel and unlikely dietary laws; there are other cynics who maintain that the proscription resulted from Mohammed's petulance over the fact that some of his soldiers had fallen to gambling, drinking, and subsequently quarreling among themselves, and had as a result narrowly escaped a thrashing at the hands of some unbelievers. Whatever the reason, the prophet promptly had some visions, duly recorded in the Sûrahs of the Koran: "They question thee about strong drink and games of chance. Say: In both is great sin, and (some) utility for men; but the sin of them is greater than their usefulness" (Sûrah II, 219). And again: "O ye who believe! Strong drink and games of chance and idols and divining arrows are only an infamy of Satan's handiwork. Leave it aside in order that ye may succeed" (Sûrah V, 90). And even in paradise the faithful, when they recline on lined couches, will find to wait on them "immortal youths, with bowls and ewers and a cup from a pure spring, wherefrom they get no aching of the head nor any madness . . ." (Sûrah LVI, 17–19), surely a cogent religious argument for any Moslem suffering from the remorse of a hangover. But drinking among Mohammedans, especially of wine, persists.

At some time of uncertain date but probably around the beginning of the Christian era, the process of distilling alcoholic beverages was developed, somewhere in the Orient. For an invention of, as some have said, the Devil, it found its way to Europe at a fairly placid pace. Spirits were not commonly available in Europe until the late 1400's. Once introduced, they began, at least in some areas, to replace beers and wines as the alcoholic beverage of choice. Wherever this happened, it had three effects. The first was that one could get drunk quicker, which to some people was undoubtedly a recommendation. The second was that the drinker could expect even greater nutritional imbalance than had been possible with beers and wines,* and the race could in consequence expect an exacerbation of health problems generally.

* The argument that there is food value in alcoholic beverages constitutes one of the supplest rationalizations in the armament of the Wets. Correspondingly, the fact that there *are* food values in alcoholic beverages constitutes one of the sharpest thorns in the hide of the Drys. Alcohol is high in caloric content but very low in nutritional value. Distillation removes vitamins from spirits. Beer and wine, which have less alcohol content than spirits, also have more nutritive elements: there are in beer traces of vitamins, but they are inconsiderable, for the present-day practice of pasteurization and filtration removes much of the food value; wine contains about the same amount of vitamins and minerals as does grape juice.

The third effect, while it was slower to make itself felt, was the most important. It was economic. This was the period, in Europe, of mercantilism, the economic policy of exporting as much as possible and importing as little as possible, in order to achieve a favorable balance of trade in gold and silver. Liquor became a government concern. Distilleries were encouraged. A part of agricultural produce—and an important part—was diverted to the distilleries. The clergy could and did inveigh against the burgeoning liquor traffic, but it had become a significant aspect of national policy. In England, for example, the drinking of spirits had increased throughout the 1600's, but the drink was Holland gin. Two students of the alcohol problem * have written:

"As a part of the English policy of gaining commercial in-

Native brews, of course, are likely to be more nutrient than our more civilized and refined product. Beer made from mare's milk, for example, will clearly have a high nutritional value. And the British biologist Haldane pointed up the ironies implicit in a report published by the Royal Medical Society Bulletin in 1930. Near the equator, in the Pacific Ocean, lies Nauru Island, mandated to the Australian government after the first World War. It is rich in phosphates, which make a useful fertilizer. The natives of Nauru had, from time immemorial, drunk a home-brew fermented from palm leaves; it got them drunk, so the Australian officials prohibited the drink so that they might better mine phosphates for the world's food supply. Infant mortality shot up from seven to fifty per cent in six months. The red-faced officials, having discovered that the cause for this tragedy was the disappearance of the B vitamins from the mothers' milk, lifted—after the usual bureaucratic delays—their prohibition. At once the infant mortality rates went down again to about seven per cent.

But this story should foster no illusions. Alcohol is a very third-rate food. Our estimation of the efficacy of alcoholic beverages regarded simply as a food may be gauged by the fact that we have tucked discussion of the subject away down here, where it is, in a footnote.

* Raymond G. McCarthy and Edgar M. Douglass, in their generally excellent *Alcohol and Social Responsibility,* in which much of their attention is focused on the needful area of public education on the problems of alcohol.

dependence, the importation of distilled liquors was prohibited in 1689. To meet the demand for spirits and at the same time sustain a policy of agricultural expansion, the establishment of distilleries was encouraged. It was possible for an individual to secure a license for a small fee and within ten days go into the distillery business. In about 1700 the granting of licenses for the retail sale of distilled spirits was introduced. There was a rapid increase in the production of spirituous liquors and it was during this first quarter of the eighteenth century that the drinking of beverages of high alcohol content greatly increased in England. This was the era of widespread gin-drinking among the poor, of drinking clubs patronized by rich young bloods, and the development of toasting and drinking rituals."

This powerful economic motive, it might be conjectured, would have surely tipped the scales of man's social ambivalence about alcohol. But an equally powerful reaction was brewing. At about the same time (1751) that the scathing British satirist, Hogarth, was printing his "Beer Street" and "Gin Lane," a savage indictment of distilled spirits, the temperance movement was forming. It got its first impetus from a religious leader, John Wesley, the Methodist, in 1753. Because organizationally it was based in a religious denomination, it quickly jumped across the Atlantic to the American colonies. And so will we.

There are a number of excellent reasons for focusing our attention on the various aspects of drinking in the United States, to the relative exclusion of habits and attitudes elsewhere. For one, the World Health Organization's figures indicate that the drinking problem is more severe in this country than elsewhere. As of 1951, it had been estimated that there were 3,952 American alcoholics with and without complications for every 100,000 adults. This compares with 2,850 French alcoholics measured on the same basis, and France has the dubious distinction of running second. Clearly, the United States is well in the lead. For another thing, in the United States there has been crystallized, over the last century and a half, the neatest continuing examples of social ambivalence toward alcohol. For a third, here in our society are combined (and, very gradually, are becoming homogeneous) a great many different cultural influences, a great many different ingrained attitudes toward alcohol. The problem is here in macrocosm.

Colonial America was no stranger to the mercantilist drives mentioned earlier. The Puritans were not abstinent to begin with, although in every settlement along the coast from Maine to Georgia habitual drunkenness was punished. But their attitudes toward drinking were the usual British attitudes: they drank ale and wine and beer, and considered that the drinking of these things assisted them in weathering their severe winters. What Holland gin did to England, rum did to the American colonies.

The triangular trade, West Indies–New England–Africa: molasses-rum-slaves, was in full swing by the early 1700's. By the 1770's it had proved to be the most profitable commercial venture the colonials had been able to develop; they considered it vital to their continuing prosperity; and rum had become an indispensable part of their social life. The town with a population of a thousand or so that did not boast its own distillery was the exception. The slogans were, expectably, Buy American and Drink American. Wages often included a daily issue of rum. By the turn of the century the new nation had cut its teeth on a bottle of spirits and, though still an infant, had bitten out the cork and was forming the habit of drinking straight, drinking deep, and drinking hard.

But once again, man's basic ambivalence toward the drug was, during this period, building up an equal head of steam. Puritan clerics conceived intemperance to be a threat to Christianity itself, and they were speaking from pulpits in a society very close to being a theocracy. The Quakers were active, also, in attacking intemperance. And, from England in 1753, there came John Wesley's Discipline. He spoke, as we have said, for an organized group which was also evangelistic, so his adjurations were calculated to be effective at once with a few, and later to spread to the many.

The Wesleyan Discipline forbade drunkenness, and enjoined the sale of spirits or their use for any except the most necessary medical reasons.* And in America his counsel was heeded from the time the news of it arrived in America.

Its effect was slow but impressive. Any notion that the Discipline would be effective only among the Methodists was wrong. Business leaders, educators, newspaper editors, physicians (notably Dr. Benjamin Rush, one of the signers of the Declaration of Independence and a man of medicine whose insights into the problems of mental health were remarkable), and congressmen joined the clergy in growing opposition to intemperance. An American Society for the Promotion of Temperance, formed in 1826, could claim a membership of 500,000 by 1833, and this from a population of only some thirteen million; the Temperance Union next year claimed 1,000,-000 members. Moreover, distilleries were closing. To the temperance forces, it seemed that victory was at hand. One of the eleven temperance journals of the time boasted that the number of American drunkards had been reduced from 200,000 to 125,000 and the number of moderate drinkers from 6,000,000 to 3,000,000.

A children's Cold Water Army was on the march. These

* Therapeutics, as a science, had not progressed very far in 1753. In fact, the medical profession today does not uniformly recommend alcoholic beverages for any ailment, psychic or somatic. Some cardiovascular specialists, but by no means all, incline to the belief that in great moderation alcoholic beverages can be helpful to elderly patients.

were the days of best-selling temperance tales like "Ten Nights in a Bar-Room" and "The Bottle and the Pledge," and even Walt Whitman took some time away from his ale at the Pewter Mug Tavern to hack a temperance yarn called "Franklin Evans; or, The Inebriate."

The temperance groups were everywhere. A movement imbued with such zeal was bound to impress politicians, and in any event there were bound to be more than a few politicians themselves zealous abstainers. From the establishment of temperance groups in state legislatures and in the national Congress to thinking how splendid it would be if a law were passed is a very short step indeed. Agitation for state and federal laws to prohibit the liquor traffic became a serious factor around 1840.

Thereafter, for the next one hundred years, the vacillation of the American people on the public question of the liquor traffic has been a most remarkable phenomenon in our national political life.

In three separate periods the cycle of prohibition-and-repeal has been repeated.

In the 1850's, following the lead of Maine, thirteen of the thirty-one states in the union passed laws prohibiting the manufacture, distribution, and sale of alcoholic beverages. But by 1863 all but one had either repealed or drastically modified its laws.

In the 1880's, eight states outlawed the traffic. But by 1904 most had repealed the laws.

A third time an attempt was made: twenty-five states were dry by 1917 and by 1919 the nation was dry. That law was repealed in 1933.

The vacillation has been explained on a number of grounds, and probably every reason adduced has some merit. There is no doubt, for example, that only the temperance groups have had consistent and effective and unified leadership. Again, much has been made of the hypocrisy implicit in the vacillation: the regularity with which politicians drank Wet and voted Dry. But to call it hypocrisy is to lend a moral cast to a deep-rooted human conflict. The tendency to drink Wet and vote Dry may be cynical; it may be also simply another expression of the basic ambivalence toward alcohol.

In the 1840's and 1850's, the temperance adherents were successful in linking their cause with other, very potent, moral issues. In those days, the same speakers used to turn up regularly on platforms calling for prohibition, women's rights, public education, and the abolition of slavery. They were charged with radicalism, they were taunted with epithets like Humbug, Old Fogy, Pantaloon, Black Bloomer, and so on, but the weight of moral rectitude was with them. They could survive even the unwelcome appearance in their camp, briefly, of the Know-Nothings. These bigots, dedicated to opposition to the waves of immigration from Europe, managed to lug the liquor question into their malodorous politicking: the Irish immigrant was caricatured as a keg of whisky, the German immigrant as a barrel of beer, and both portrayed as stealing the ballot box.

A presidential election was lost, it has always been supposed, when a Republican preacher let fall the fatal phrase, "Rum, Romanism, and Rebellion." That was in the 1880's, and while the remark might have found approval in the temperance states of the Midwest, the notion will not down that it cost the Republicans the state of New York and the election.

Similar myths obtain as to the Volstead Act of 1919. There seem always to be special reasons why prohibitory laws succeed. In this case, the claim is that it could never have passed had "our boys" not been "over there" fighting a war on foreign shores. But the case was by no means so simple. The Anti-Saloon League and the Women's Christian Temperance Union had been persistently lobbying in Congress for forty years; their grass-roots strength was impressive. The amendment was passed by the Congress in 1917 not because a significant section of the American population was overseas but because there was no comparable articulate, organized, and zealous force in the country to oppose it.

The vacillation has, of course, by no means come to a stop simply because the Eighteenth Amendment was repealed. It will never stop. Despite Repeal, there are two states—Oklahoma and Mississippi *—that are legally dry. In addition, however, it is estimated that some twenty million Americans living in twenty-nine other states cannot buy a legal drink in their home neighborhood. This is the result of local-option laws. In Ohio, for example, as of 1954, 422 townships were bone-dry, in 417 townships liquor could be sold only from package stores, and the other 521 townships were still wet. For their part, the distillers mourn. They use phrases like "creeping prohibition," and they are not sure but what the whole Dry effort is not perhaps some sort of plot, vaguely un-American. One distiller has said: "The Drys operate like Communists. They infiltrate a weak spot and take over. That's what's happening right now all over the country."

In one sense, the distiller can be worried: man will never wholly approve of drinking. In another sense, he can sleep easy: man will never wholly approve of abstinence. It is our ambivalence, the basic conflict in our emotional attitudes toward alcohol, that is chiefly responsible for the political vacil-

---

* A curious situation exists in Mississippi. The state treasurer annually includes, as part of his statement of receipts, an item covering taxes on black-market liquor. The state is technically dry. Nevertheless, if a liquor distributor wishes to transport, say, two truckloads of whisky from Memphis to Biloxi, he will be informed by a friendly authority over which roads his trucks should move and at which hours, and he will pay an *ad valorem* tax on his shipment.

lations of the last century or so; and it is reasonable to expect that the same ambivalence will continue to disturb our thinking and confuse our actions and color our attitudes for at least the next century.

Only the satirist dares predict otherwise. Aldous Huxley described, in his *Brave New World*, the perfect drug. He called it soma. Two thousand pharmacologists and biochemists were subsidized to develop it; it was "euphoric, narcotic, pleasantly hallucinant," having "all the advantages of Christianity and alcohol, but none of their defects." Thanks to soma, "Stability was practically assured. . . . It only remained to conquer old age."

But that is the reality of satire. Our vision is limited to a sadder and more humdrum reality. Our drug is less than perfect, nor does it lend us stability. We are stuck with it, and we are stuck, too, with our conflicts about it.

III

And so here we are, back again at the big numbers with which we launched this inquiry, the numbers that describe our consumption of alcoholic beverages in 1954: 189,000,000 gallons of distilled spirits, 2,557,000,000 gallons of beer and ale, and 176,-000,000 gallons of wine. These impressive totals have been always in the back of our minds as we traced, very sketchily, some of the aspects of our drinking habits. But now it is time we inspected them close up.

For a start, let us examine a handful of statistical generalizations about the drinkers who put all this liquor away. Like all generalizations, these must be handled with caution and interpreted only with suspicion. For, as always with statistics, anything can be done with them. They can be used, after combing them selectively, to prove that drinking in America is spreading in alarming fashion; or they can be used to shore up the contention that our national drinking mores are far more relaxed and sensible than ever before. Where is the truth? As usual, there is a little of it lurking shyly behind each conclusion.

One danger lies in the term *drinker*. Since it includes both the alcoholic off on a roaring wingding and your Aunt Mildred who once a year at Christmas wets her lips with a brandy eggnog as part of a family ceremony, a statement about drinkers may be entirely valid but at the same time flagrantly tendentious.

Moreover, in a country so big, so sprawling, so diffused with various and conflicting folkways and customs, to set down national averages is to deal in meaningless symbols, no matter if they seem to speak with the authority of the Last Trump. Nevertheless:

About two out of every three Americans fifteen years and older drink alcoholic beverages in some form.* Of these, forty

* The statistical estimates of drinkers and drinking habits come from two independent studies and, since in substance the data of each survey coincide with and corroborate those of the other, we are not troubling to particularize. One, to which we have already referred, is the 1946 study made by John W. Riley, Jr. and Charles F. Marden, of Rutgers University. The other is the continuing study made by the American Institute of Public Opinion (the Gallup Poll), from 1946 to 1952.

The percentage differences, from study to study and from year to year, are not significant when allowance is made for the size of samples and so on. The key statistic, for example, is the one determining the number of those who drink and the number of those who abstain. The Rutgers survey stated this ratio to be 65–35. The Gallup polls have come up with findings that vary from 67–33 to 58–42. It would seem reasonable to strike an average, and conclude that something like sixty-three or sixty-four per cent of us drink. Both these studies ignored the older teen-agers. But as we have already pointed out, there is ample evidence to demonstrate that the drinking population should be computed on the basis of all those fifteen years old and up.

per cent may be considered regular drinkers, in the sense that they take anywhere from a few drinks a week to one or more drinks a day. Another forty per cent drink once or twice a month. The others are truly only occasional drinkers.

There were in 1954 114,000,000 Americans at least fifteen years old. It is safe to say that 70,000,000 of them shared in drinking the year's grand total of alcoholic beverages.

The chief comment to make on this figure is that it has grown enormously in the past fifteen years. In 1940, Dr. Jellinek estimated the drinking population—and his informed guess was generally accepted by all authorities—at forty-four million. For this group to have jumped nearly sixty-three per cent in fifteen years says much about the social pressures working within our national population. The expectable increase, taking into consideration only the normal population rise over the same period, would have been about fifty-four per cent.

Three out of four men drink. A little more than half the women drink. Three times as many men as women drink regularly—that is, at least three times a week.

A quarter-century ago the gap between the number of men and women drinkers was much greater; a century ago it was greater still, the woman drinker was a rarity; and it may be hazarded that a quarter-century from now the gap will have even further diminished. As the sociologists concerned with the Rutgers survey remarked: "This narrowing of the gap between the sexes in respect to drinking would appear to be in line with the general trend of our society toward less and less differentiation in the social behavior of men and women."

There are twice as many Protestant abstainers (forty-one per cent) as there are Catholic abstainers (twenty-one per cent) and thrice as many as there are Jewish abstainers (thirteen per cent).

This is almost wholly misleading. It serves no purpose to

lump all the Protestants together, for they derive from entirely different cultural backgrounds. Their attitudes toward alcohol range all the way from the rigid Dry prohibitionism of the evangelistic Bible Belt to the casual permissiveness of the Episcopalians of the urban northeastern states. Turning to Catholicism, when we think of the Catholic congregation in this country, rightly or wrongly we think first of the Irish-Americans and the Italian-Americans. But the two can by no means be fitted into the same category in terms of alcohol. There are relatively few abstainers in either group, but there are more alcoholics among the Americans of Irish descent, proportionally, than among those of any other ethnic grouping, while there are fewer alcoholics, proportionally, among the Americans of Italian descent than among any others save the Jews. As for the Jews, the wonder is that the investigators found such a high percentage (thirteen) of Jewish abstainers, for wine is part and parcel of Jewish religious and social ritual. Wine is drunk at the Sabbath service, at the Passover celebration, and on many other occasions. On the other hand, despite the relative rarity of the Jewish abstainer, the incidence of alcoholism among the Jewish people is, by every test, the lowest in the country. Nevertheless, attitudes toward alcoholic beverages among American Jewry are various and constantly undergoing further change. There is the Orthodox attitude, which requires strict adherence to ancient ritualistic laws; there is the Conservative attitude, which regards those laws rather more permissively; there is the Reform attitude, which is comparatively cavalier about the letter of Hebraic law; and of course among secular Jews the disposition is to regard alcoholic beverages quite as the rest of the community does. Additionally, it seems unwarranted to erect any religious categories. In our time, Americans are inured to categorization: automatically, they will say—to a poll-taker, to a sociologist, to a draft-board, to whomever—that they belong to this or that religious category, simply as a convenience, simply because they happened to have been born into it. Their answer may have nothing to do with the fact. They may be, by conviction and by behavior, entirely secular. The effect of their response is to impute to the congregation they have left long since an irresponsibility toward alcohol, alcoholism, and inebriety which is, to say the least, an inconvenience.

Finally, every fact adduced in the paragraphs above about an ethnic or a religious group has undergone change since the time questions were asked and answers given; indeed, each has probably undergone change between the time the statement was written and the time you read it; and there is every likelihood that the change, in each case, has worked in the direction of further blurring the distinctions.

Here are some more statistical generalizations:

The number of drinkers grows steadily in proportion to the size of the population in the community: from forty-six per cent in the rural farm areas to seventy-seven per cent in the largest cities.

The higher the economic level, the higher the percentage of drinkers.

The higher the educational level, the higher the percentage both of moderate drinkers and of regular drinkers.

But it is a matter of common observation that in the American national community the habits and tastes of the urban, the better-educated, and the well-to-do tend to pervade the rest of the community. They are precisely the style-setters, the fashion-molders, the market-leaders. We are impelled to the conclusion, once again, that as time goes on distinctions postulated on these bases will blur.

We are permitted to infer, then, that the substantial increase in the drinking population which has come about in the last ten or fifteen years has drawn its recruits from every segment of the national population, without regard to sex, income, religion, educational level, age, or whatever else; and that in the process of growth the differences that formerly set the drinking groups apart from the abstaining groups are tending to disappear—that is, where once abstainers were in the majority or were a significant minority, that is no longer the case or tends to be less the case.

There are more of us drinking than ever before. Are those of us who drink also drinking more, and harder? To be sure, the total product of the liquor industry has substantially and steadily increased ever since Repeal, but is that not to be attributed to the normal increase in population and the rather greater increase in the number of drinkers?

There are many ways of estimating the rate of liquor consumption. The distillers, for example, somewhat disingenuously point out that consumption of spirits in 1850 was 5.57 gallons per capita of the adult population, that by 1860 it had reached 6.92 gallons per capita, while in 1953 it was away down to a sober 1.94 gallons per capita—a trivial amount, about three 1.5-ounce drinks a week. Such an approach is misleading. In the hands of the distillers it becomes evidence to support the argument that taxes on spirits should be cut. As such, it does not convince, but it does help to prove something quite different and far more important, as we shall see in a moment.

A more accurate standard for estimating the rate of liquor consumption is to measure it in terms of the consumption of absolute alcohol (whether in spirits, in wine, or in beer), divided per capita among all those at least fifteen years old. And now there emerges a quite fascinating fact:

1850	2.07 gallons per capita
1950	2.04 gallons per capita
1953	1.99 gallons per capita
1954	1.93 gallons per capita

Over a century and more, this figure has maintained a remarkable consistency. As the population has shifted and grown, so also has the consumption of absolute alcohol. Much the same consistency is evident if the absolute alcohol is divided amongst only the drinkers. Here we have not available so wide a range for comparative purposes, for it was not until 1940 that any careful attempt was made to count the heads of the drinking population.

1940	44,000,000 drinkers	3.59 gallons per capita
1950	65,000,000 drinkers	3.45 gallons per capita
1953	67,500,000 drinkers	3.41 gallons per capita
1954	70,000,000 drinkers	3.29 gallons per capita

So, while more of us are drinking, it would seem we are drinking less per capita. And now the significance of the figures cited earlier by the distillers becomes obvious: a revolution in American drinking habits has taken place in the last century, and especially since Repeal: we have changed from a nation of relatively few drinkers who drank hard, to a nation of many drinkers who drink less and more lightly. There is far more beer and wine in our shopping baskets and in our refrigerators than ever before.

To some extent, this radical shift is a reflection of the changing ethnic composition of the population. The immigrants from Europe brought with them and have since clung to their preference for wine and beer over spirits. But, in addition, those preferences have been contagious. Typically, a survey for the Wine Institute in 1952 showed that more than one of every four wine-drinking families had picked up the habit only since 1946. And again, while the sale of distilled spirits has risen since 1940, it has done so jerkily, yielding ground every so often; but the sale of beer and wine has been almost uniformly on the increase. As a nation, we now drink more absolute alcohol in our beer than we do in our spirits.

But all this discussion relates only to the legal product. Any estimate of our total consumption of alcoholic beverages must take the bootleg traffic into account. Obviously, it is impossible to cite any accurate and authoritative estimate of the amount of moonshine that slides down American throats. But an informed guess is possible.

Bootleggers are, broadly, of two kinds.

In the South there is the informal moonshiner, an amateur, a man who, with his five- to fifty-gallon pot still, contrives to turn out a modest amount of liquor, usually corn whisky, usually raw and hot, sometimes superb drinking whisky. He operates, more often than not, in the off-hours from some other, more legal occupation. He distills his brew in Georgia, and in Kentucky, and in Tennessee, and in Mississippi, and in Alabama, and elsewhere as well, but those, in that order, are the states with the most impressive and most regular output. He sells his product over the back fence to his neighbors and to his neighbors' friends, and in addition he hopes to make a tie-in with illicit distributors who can in turn work his product into the Northern market. It is an open question how often he is able to do so. There are a great many stories, most of them touched with romance, of powerful, high-speed black limousines and sedans, their springs creaking under their heavy loads of moonshine, roaring around the mountainous, hairpin curves of Kentucky and West Virginia in flight from the revenue agents, on their way north to Chicago or Detroit. There is quite probably a modicum of truth in these tales.

In the North, the bootlegger is a different breed of cat. He is a professional. He operates a continuous-process or column-pot still, capable of far greater production than the Southern pot still. He is, by and large, the same man who was doing the same thing years ago, during Prohibition, and, in consequence, he is as familiar to the Internal Revenue Service as the fur thief is to a big city's Loft Squad. This means that the Service's agents need only check on him, from time to time, during his regular and predictable periods of freedom from prison, in order to find out what he is doing at the moment. He is an old friend. He does not distill potable liquor. His product (and it is very good; he is quite proud of it) is 180-proof or even 190-proof alcohol. He sells to one or more illegal distributors who in turn sell to individuals or speakeasies. The buyer gets a five-gallon tin. If the buyer is an individual, he busies himself adding water and flavoring matter to his alcohol to make it potable at his own preferred strength. If the buyer is a speakeasy, the alcohol will probably be cut to 60-proof and sold straight. There are many American drinkers who prefer precisely such a potent draught.*

Of one thing the Internal Revenue Service agents are positive: the illicit product of the North never finds its way into legal distribution channels and is never sold across the bar or counter of a legally licensed establishment.

Perhaps the best way of judging how extensive is the bootleg traffic is to observe the trend in Federal still seizures. In the twenty months ending on February 28, 1955, stills were raided at the rate of one thousand a month. Most of them were small.

---

* Such speakeasies, these days, are usually temporary affairs housed in the apartments of tenements in the poorer neighborhoods of large cities. Nor is 60-proof alcohol the only illicit commodity for sale. In New York City's Harlem, some detectives of the Narcotics Squad had occasion to raid, in May, 1955, one such speakeasy. The man who answered their knock at the door, unaware of their identity, asked them: "You want to flip, flap, or fly?" Thus pungently, he was offering them their choice of bootleg alcohol, the services of a prostitute, or narcotics.

There were only some seventy-odd big continuous-process or column-pot stills seized.* Back in 1939-40, over a comparable period, more than three hundred of these large-capacity stills were seized. Nevertheless, we must not sneer at the recent seizures: the *daily* production capacity of the stills raided during those twenty months was more than three hundred thousand gallons. And a conservative rule-of-thumb runs: "For every still seized, there is another in operation." The question is: For how long?

Clearly, the profit motive is one that tempts the would-be bootlegger most winningly. Taxes give him a competitive edge of better than two dollars on each fifth of whisky. Industrial empires have been built on less. His only enemies are Federal vigilance and industry pressure. For their part, government officials flatly refuse to venture how much moonshine reaches the market. Industry spokesmen are not so bashful. They contend their criminal competition turned out sixty-eight million gallons in 1954. We may regard their estimate as prejudiced. A wiser guess would put the total at between twenty-five and thirty million gallons a year.

It is in any event an impressive dollop of contraband liquor,

* In the late spring of 1955, Internal Revenue agents seized a huge still in a desolate section of Brooklyn, a plant described by one of the agents as "the largest column type cooker I have ever seen." Its capacity was 600 gallons of 190-proof alcohol every twelve hours. It had been in operation for three months. Tax losses to the government were variously estimated at $20,000 a day to $2,000,000 for the three-month period. Seized were seventeen vats filled with 60,000 gallons of mash, 125 five-gallon cans of alcohol ready for distribution, 1,000 empty cans, 3,600 pounds of sugar, 100 bags of yeast, and several thousand empty sugar bags.

Cost of the equipment was estimated at $50,000. The bootlegger was able to get about $26 for a five-gallon can of alcohol. After diluting this to half its strength, the distributor was able to sell the ten gallons for $70. Over a three-month period the manufacturers might well have realized $500,000 on their investment; the distributors were estimated to have realized $1,500,000, a tidy profit.

and one which requires us to revise our earlier arithmetic on per capita consumption for 1954 like this:

70,000,000 drinkers   3.48 gallons per capita

There has been a steady increase, over the last ten years, in the amount of illicit spirits seized. This is suggestive. It would seem to indicate that the bootleg business is getting bigger. This is most decidedly not evidence of the kind that can be taken into a court, but it is nevertheless sufficient to enable us to dare draw a conclusion. On the basis of our earlier arithmetic we said it would seem we are drinking less per capita. But taking into consideration the growing bootleg traffic, we conclude that not only are more of us drinking but we are also drinking more per capita. Because, however, so much of our consumption of absolute alcohol is in the form of beer and wine, the national trend is toward greater temperance.

The first half of our conclusion, that more of us are drinking, is valid beyond a cavil. The second half, that we are likewise drinking more per capita, is questionable. It cannot be proved; it cannot be disproved. As with almost every flat-footed statement that anyone can make about a matter involving alcohol, it will find its vehement attackers and defenders. In fact, however, it does not seem to matter too much whether it is accurate or not. In either event, there will be those among the drinkers who should not, for their own health and the health of society, drink a drop. For them, the substance is poison.

Indeed, among the dwindling group of abstainers there are those for whom the substance would also be poison, should they ever be moved, by whatever social or personal pressure, to abandon their abstemiousness. Among the teen-agers who have not yet experimented with the substance, there are predictably and positively those who will learn to their dismay that it is poison. Is *poison* too emotional a word? Here at hand is a newspaper clipping. It tells of how two husky teen-age youths celebrated the eighteenth birthday of one. Before their party was over they had stolen three cars, pistol-whipped six men about the head, and nearly killed a seventh. They were "emboldened" to these deeds, so runs the report, by having drunk boilermakers, that is to say, whisky with beer chasers.

Among seventy million drinkers there are, of course, sure to be an appreciable number of fools and sick men. It can be assumed that there will be a larger number of fools and sick men in 1960, when the population of drinkers will have to some extent grown, and a still larger number in 1965, and so on.

For the drinking population will certainly grow larger. The pressures working to insure its growth are fixed and will be maintained. We have already touched on the most forceful of those pressures, but there are others.

Consider, for example, the simple fact that the legal alcoholic beverage industry is a significant factor in the American economy and quite naturally seeks an ever-expanding market. It is big: it provides employment for 1,200,000 Americans, pays in wages and salaries and dividends an annual $3,200,000,000, represents a capital investment of nearly $9,000,000,000, and spends at least $130,000,000 every year to persuade us to buy more of its product.

Its advertising agents sing their usual siren song. Listen: "Best-tasting . . . new and exciting pleasures . . . smooth, easy to take, the only thing that lingers on is the pleasant memory . . . among the better things of life . . . incomparable pleasure . . . both age and nobility . . . the crest of quality . . . liquid gold . . . renowned, most cherished . . . connoisseurs prefer . . . discriminating taste . . . It's always a pleasure! . . . Live better today than ever before . . . smart vogue . . . discerning hosts and hostesses always serve . . .

traditionally correct . . . the choice of those who could command the finest . . . product of genius . . . mellower, smoother, tastier, milder . . . If you have expensive tastes . . . intended solely for those people with a flair for elegance and the means to afford it . . . for fashionable people . . ." *

And buy their product we do: $10 billion worth in 1954, of which sum $4 billion went to Federal, state, and local governments.

Would one more statistic come amiss? The distillers annually turn over to the National Research Council $45,000—no strings attached—to help support scientific research in the problems of alcoholism.

How to assess the social phenomenon of American drinking? How to evaluate something that spells cheer and good fellowship to so many and at the same time misery to so many others? How to measure whether, ultimately, this magic substance, this poison, this drug, this narcotic, this pleasant beverage is helping or hindering us on our tortuous journey to tomorrow?

This much can be said. We have not accepted alcohol as an integrated part of our culture. We are still in sharp conflict about it. Our ambivalence is deep-rooted. In the widest social sense and in the deepest individual sense it seems likely that this conflict will always rule.

In terms of the last century, the trend has been toward temperance. In societies where temperance is the rule, it follows that drinking is at once milder but more widespread. And when more people drink, it follows inexorably that there are more people drinking who should not.

That is and will be the case among us.

* This cupful of blood, sweat and tears from Madison Avenue was squeezed out of three issues of *The New Yorker.*

Some of us shouldn't

I

The bedside phone rang, waking the doctor up, and, as she flicked on the light, she was annoyed with herself for not having switched off the phone, so that her answering service might have attended to the call.

It was, she saw, nearly four in the morning.

The voice that said, "Hello, doctor," was drunken.

She told her caller that she would see him at ten that morning, turned over, and went back to sleep, reflecting that he would never come. They almost never follow through, these early-hour, impulsive, impatient drinkers, with whom self-reproach has made an unexpected and unwelcome appointment. But at ten that morning he was waiting in her reception room.

He was a young man, perhaps twenty-seven. He was in a hurry. He resented the fact that the doctor was two or three minutes late. He said he had heard that she had a pill that would stop him from drinking.

She explained that, as she uses it, the pill called Antabuse is only an adjunct to psychotherapy.

He scowled.

She went on to say that she would like him to come inside to her office; that she would like to talk to him, find out more about him, help him to find out more about himself, work with him to find out why he felt he had a problem about alcohol.

His scowl cut deeper, and he fetched an elaborately impatient sigh, but he followed her into her office.

She told him she was impressed with the fact that he had shown up at her office. It showed, she said, that he was truly interested in getting well.

"It's because I want one of your pills," he said irritably. "That's all I need. I've just got to stay sober."

The doctor considered. At length she gave him some Antabuse, instructing him at the same time as to how he should use it, what he could expect of it, what purpose it should serve him.* She told him she wanted him to come back in a week's time. Then once again she introduced the subject of supportive therapy.

"You act as though I was some kind of a nut," the young man said, querulously. "You think I'm neurotic? I don't need any psychotherapy! Look. All I want is these pills, I can't get them without a prescription, and you want me to come back, lie down on a couch, and tell you all about my sex life! Who's crazy?"

"I didn't," said the doctor, "say anything about your sex life."

"No, but you said psychotherapy. It's the same thing, isn't it?" The young man reached for his hat. "Thanks for the pills," he said. "Just because I drink too much, just because

* The role of Antabuse in the therapy of alcoholism is discussed at length on page 174.

71

I've got to stay sober for a while," and he was angry now, "you want to make me out a neurotic or something! Not for me, thank you very much! Goodbye!"

"I'll be seeing you," said the doctor.

As her door slammed she considered (for perhaps the hundredth time) how man, when he began speculating about science and nature, had first examined the stars, because they were farthest away from him. Later he tackled physics and chemistry; still later biology; anatomy and physiology are still his very present concerns. But psychology? The scientific study of what we think and why, and what we feel and why? That cuts too close to where man lives. Here all is still magic, still tainted by the sorcery of the witch-doctor and the medicine-man. His patients call a psychiatrist head-squeezer or head-shrinker when they are more polite; and they at least have overcome their resistance to the point of becoming his patients. What do they call him, how much do they fear him, who will not suffer him to help them?

His province is our mental life, his task to help us overcome our mental ailments, and one of his greatest handicaps the stigma that attaches to all mental illness. Such a stigma has in the past affected (and to some extent still affects) the treatment of other diseases—cancer and tuberculosis come to mind, and the venereal diseases—but not to nearly the same extent as is the case with mental illness. What the stigma has meant for the seriously ill is quite horrible. Our ancestors feared the "madman" and killed him; our grandfathers, more humane, threw him in irons and hid him away in appalling prisons called asylums, from which indeed he has not yet been wholly freed. But we have learned, in the light of science, that the term *madman* is silly, and as our knowledge of the psychoses grows the stigma has begun to fade.

But shame and fear still attach, profoundly and tenaciously, to the milder mental ailments. It is ingrained in us that we should be brave and self-reliant, that we should be able to handle our problems, that we should snap out of it if we feel depressed, that we should keep our chin up, keep smiling. To be neurotic, to fall prey to hysteria or anxiety, is to be a sissy, a coward, a weakling. It is to invite the phrase *Something is wrong with him*, or *She's different*, or *He's queer*, at a time and in a society in which conformity, being liked and being like, is the ruling must.

The stigma governs absolutely. The sickness—even talk about it—is taboo. And a psychiatrist, Flanders Dunbar, after studying army and industrial records, concluded that eighty per cent of the American population need psychiatric help. Our shame and our fear hoot at such a judgment. But our society sickens.

What has all this to do with alcoholism? This: there is a disposition to seek to classify alcoholism as a disease which is in some way physiological. It is claimed to be the result of a dysfunction of metabolism, or of heredity, or of nutrition, or of the endocrine glands, or of this, that, or the other constitutional factor. Doctors as well as laymen strive to argue these conclusions; alcoholics pitiably share in the delusion.

For delusion it is.

Alcoholism is a neurosis.

Technically, it is classified as a psychoneurosis and subclassified as an impulse neurosis. It may appear in conjunction with an ailment of some other kind and thus offer a more complicated diagnostic problem. Such another ailment, while usually also mental, is sometimes physical. But alcoholism itself is a neurosis.

Despite all the efforts to demonstrate that alcoholism results from some constitutional deficiency, despite all the hopes and wishes of the alcoholics themselves that somehow they may

73

escape from the stigma of neurosis, alcoholism is a mental illness.

What purpose is served the sick by holding out to them the false hope that some day some physiological "x-factor" will be discovered, as a magical result of which they will all be well? They are better served by being helped to understand that what ails them has to do with their personality structure, that they are by no means to blame, that there is nothing morally or socially reprehensible about their alcoholism. Good, bad, right, wrong, strength, weakness—these concepts have nothing to do with their sickness. As sick people they are, if Flanders Dunbar is right, in the majority. (And we believe she is, in any event, not far wrong.) The only thing that is special, then, about the alcoholics is the nature of their symptom. As to that, it can be arrested. It is not too much to say that it can be cured, although admittedly the number of those who have been completely cured, so that they may resume social controlled drinking, does not to date exceed the number of fingers on one hand. But if more alcoholics are to be cured, the first step will have been taken when there is recognition that alcoholism is a neurosis.

The tragedy is only that this should be regarded as a tragedy. To be sure, at the present stage of our knowledge, a mental illness is more difficult to treat than such a physical illness as, say, chickenpox, but the individual with a neurosis is no more to blame, no more to be shunned, has no more reason to feel guilty or ashamed, than the individual with the pox itching at his face and neck and arms and chest. Doctors assume from the way in which the infecting organism of chickenpox behaves that it is a virus; but this is not known for a fact. The sickness, however, runs its course with only very rare complications; it is very easily treated. Doctors assume from the way a neurotic behaves that his sickness is the result of things that happened to him in his interpersonal relationships, and most probably in his infancy or childhood; but this is not known for an indisputable fact. The sickness can, however, be arrested, treated, and, in the case of many neuroses, often cured. What is the difference? Etiologically, each is to some extent obscure. Therapeutically, chickenpox is a cinch, neurosis quite often is not. That is one difference: and a chief reason for that difference is that the whole strength of medicine was for a time directed precisely at such infectious diseases as chickenpox, while the neuroses have been the target of only a small part of medicine for only, thus far, half a century.

We have stated, flatly and arbitrarily, that alcoholism is a psychoneurosis, an impulse neurosis. We do not intend to leave the statement standing naked and undefended. We propose to demonstrate the validity of the statement and, further, we propose to examine the etiology of the ailment, that is to say, how it comes about. But first, in the interests of clearing the ground, we should establish the difference between what is healthy and what is sick, between what is normal and what is neurotic.

The difference can be likened to that between freedom and slavery. If, in the face of a given situation, you react flexibly, responding to the situation's realities, learning from experience, then you are healthy, at least in relation to such a situation. If, on the other hand, you react always in the same way, never adapting, never changing, never learning from experience, if your response is in a fixed pattern no matter what the situation's realities, then you are in trouble.

Let us put the matter more concretely. Suppose a boss reprimands a subordinate. He has done so fairly frequently before and, we shall suppose, without cause. The normal person will react to such a repeated situation in any of various ways. He may decide now to keep his mouth shut, now to answer back politely, now to apologize, now to retort sharply, now to ignore the whole affair, now to quit his job on the spot. Emotionally he may react with calm, with suppressed anger, with open anger, with pity, with amusement, with astonishment, or with real concern. His various emotions may have varying degrees of intensity. His particular reaction will, presumably, reflect the realities of the situation. But the point is he has a choice, and knows enough to select the appropriate emotion, the fitting phrase, the timely impulse. He is free.

The neurotic, on the other hand, is circumscribed. He is lucky if he can find more than one way to act. Perhaps he will react with panic or dismay, no matter how well he knows his boss to be in the wrong. Perhaps he will react with anger, or impatience, or insolence, no matter how often the same situation may have arisen in the past—that is to say, no matter how often he has had the opportunity to learn that the boss's wrath is temporary and probably meaningless. He is, in short, the prisoner of reactions so fixed, so frozen, so rigid as to seem almost automatic. For whatever his reaction, it will always be the same.

We can take this man a step further. We can assume that his inflexible emotional reaction has twice led to his being fired, and now a third boss presumes to take him to task. We say: Surely by now he has learned, surely now he will know better than to react with ill-concealed hostility, surely he has learned from experience to hold his tongue. But he cannot help himself. His reaction overwhelms him. He is its slave.

If the individual can learn that the consequence of his action may be hurtful, or that his impulse is futile, or that his emotion will bring only pain to himself and to those around him, and, having learned, can do or feel or think otherwise when confronted later by the same sort of situation, then he is sensible, normal, and healthy.

If the individual cannot learn, cannot understand that his

impulse or his action or his emotional attitude is going to betray him and, so far from protecting his best interests, is on the contrary going to prejudice his health or his happiness, then he is neurotic.

In so stipulating, we are not entering a moral judgment but only describing the objective clinical conclusion of every psychiatrist.

What makes the one free and enslaves the other? What—when we ask each to face the same situation—guarantees that the action of the one will be normal and the *same* action of the other be abnormal?

Clinging to our same example, let us assume that each has been unfairly criticized by his boss and that each now reacts by losing his temper. In the case of the healthy subordinate, we can predict that he has lost his temper only after having fairly tried other, more socially acceptable reactions. Having exercised his free choice and found it unavailing, he has at length reacted with anger. Further, we may guess that he knew, before permitting himself to speak sharply, that he would be able to find another, comparable job somewhere else, or at the least that his confidence that he could do so was high.

But the neurotic, as we have seen, reacts without regard for his chances of getting another job, without regard for the reality or the triviality of his boss's rage, without regard for his tenure or security, without regard for the effectiveness in such a situation of his losing his temper. He simply reacts. He simply loses his temper. His emotion is ungovernable. He does not understand it, but it happens.

Has each expression of temper gone through the same process, and come from the same part of the mind, driven by the same forces? Psychiatrists say not, and persuasively. They say that when the conscious content of the mind makes any considerable contribution to the determination of the action, the consequent behavior will be normal and healthy; but if the unconscious content of the mind makes any considerable contribution, the behavior will be abnormal and neurotic. It is an important distinction, and was first stated by Lawrence S. Kubie: *

"Wherever an alliance of the conscious and preconscious [that is, what can usually be recalled by an act of disciplined attention] systems predominates in the production of behavior, the resultant behavior will come to rest either when its goal is achieved and satiety is attained, or when the goal is found to be unattainable or ungratifying or both, whereupon the effort ceases. Thus, such behavior never becomes either insatiable or stereotyped. It can be altered by the experience of success and failure, of rewards and punishments, of pleasure and pain. It can be used to test reality and it can be tested against reality. It is therefore anchored in reality, yet it remains freely flexible. On the contrary, whenever the unconscious system (or perhaps an alliance between the preconscious and unconscious systems) predominates, the resultant action must be repeated endlessly. This occurs because its goals are predominantly unconscious symbols, and unconscious symbolic goals are never attainable. Since the predominant forces are unconscious, they will not be responsive to the experience of pleasure or of pain, or to rewards and punishments, or to logical argument—neither to the logic of events, nor to any appeals to mind or heart. The behavior that results from a dominance of the unconscious system has the insatiability, the automaticity, and the endless repetitiveness that are the stamp of the neurotic process. . . ."

Dr. Kubie, when he wrote those lines, was not attempting to describe the behavior of the alcoholic, except perhaps inciden-

* Dr. Kubie is a distinguished psychoanalyst, a former president of the New York Psychoanalytic Society, and the author of several books and many monographs.

tally. But that, when he described the neurotic, is what he has done.

To his description of the neurotic process, we may add from Otto Fenichel: * "In all neurotic symptoms something happens which the patient experiences as strange and unintelligible. This something may be . . . an overwhelming and unjustified emotion or mood. . . . All symptoms give the impression of a something that seems to break in upon the personality from an unknown source—a something that disturbs the continuity of the personality and that is outside the realm of the conscious will."

And here again there has been delineated a common experience of alcoholics.

And now, to clinch the matter, let us look at the description of an alcoholic as formulated by Marty Mann.† In her excellent *Primer on Alcoholism*, she gives a simple, practical definition of an alcoholic which, she writes, "has been [successful] in helping alcoholics to recognize their own illness." Here it is:

"An alcoholic is someone whose drinking causes a continuing problem in any department of his life." And she goes on: "The reasoning behind this definition . . . is as simple as the definition itself: if drinking is causing a continuing problem in any department of a normal or social drinker's life, he will either cut down or cut out the drinking. That is the logical and normal solution to the problem, and for a normal drinker would present no great difficulty, even though he might intensely dislike or resent having to do it. But if the drinker is an alcoholic, he may equally well realize that that is the solution;

---

* Dr. Fenichel's *The Psychoanalytic Theory of Neurosis* is a widely accepted textbook of psychoanalytic theory and practice.
† Mrs. Mann is executive director of the National Committee on Alcoholism, is herself a recovered alcoholic, and is widely experienced and respected in the field.

he may even say so, and be convinced that he is going to do it; but he won't do it, because he won't be able to do it."

Mrs. Mann has restated, in terms that introduce the concept of problem drinking in place of that of neurosis, substantially the same clinical picture as that described by Dr. Kubie.

And now it becomes clear what a callous and grievous injustice is being done the alcoholic by characterizing him as weak, or weak-willed, or cowardly. It is the fact that the alcoholic, typically, is called on to and does display far more courage in opposing his neurotic symptom, his addiction to drink, than may ever be required of the non-alcoholic. The non-alcoholic can have no conception of this kind of courage. It is often the greater precisely because it is enlisted in a losing battle. Some alcoholics can be fairly said to have accomplished heroic acts of courage in the fight against their unconscious impulses; and it is only a measure of the power of those impulses that their courage goes for nothing.

It is now time to inquire: Who is the problem drinker? How can he be recognized? And how, if possible, can he be singled out before his symptom has overwhelmed him? Is there, in short, any particular personality type that is uniquely characteristic of the alcoholic?

There are two ordinary ways of coming at this question, and each has its inadequacies. The psychologist uses projection tests, in which the individual is asked to complete sentences, associate words, draw pictures, interpret designs or ink-blots, and so on. Since the tests are standardized, the individual projects into them his own experiences, his own feelings and fantasies and thoughts and ideas. Thereupon a picture—or at least a profile—of the individual's personality emerges, to be interpreted and assessed by the psychologist. The psychiatrist, on the other hand, depends on his diagnostic ability, and infers from a series of alcoholic patients what similarities of character structure he can.

Both approaches have in the past suffered from the fact that each interested scientist has had so few examples on which to draw. One hundred alcoholics in the group to be studied is, in terms of the testing experience, a large number; but from the standpoint of statistical projection it is trivial, unless striking similarities emerge and can be found in the overwhelming preponderance of cases studied. Many of the psychological surveys can be faulted, too, on the grounds of inadequacy of controls. Moreover, to consider the psychiatric approach for a moment, here all stands or falls in direct relationship to the diagnostic ability of the physician. Additionally, terms are by no means uniform. One psychiatrist will establish categories deemed improper or inadequate by another. The classification of psychopathic personality leaps to mind: this term is an ill-defined catchall, in the hands of many clinicians, for any disturbed and poorly organized individual who does not invite classification under some more rigorously discrete heading.

These considerations have not, however, kept the psychologists and the psychiatrists from trying. There have been dozens of attempts to establish a clear and specific picture of the alcoholic personality and, by far the more difficult job, of the pre-alcoholic personality. The fair-minded reader who sets out to analyze an appreciable number of the reports of these attempts will come away with two conflicting impressions.

On the one hand, the investigators vie with each other in denying that there is such a thing as the alcoholic or pre-alcoholic personality. The more they test or diagnose, the more convinced they are (or remain) that the alcoholic is as various as man. And man, if he is nothing else, is various.

They describe him in many terms. They attribute to him many characteristics. These will include low self-esteem, self-pity, a tendency to self-punishment, resentment, a disposition to project the blame for his troubles to other people (his boss, his wife, his mother, and so on), a readiness to deny his illness, impatience, tension, depression, volatility of mood swings, stubbornness, anxiety, jealousy, and so on and on and on. Their list encompasses nearly every emotion and personality trait available to man.

On the other hand, with something close to unanimity, the investigators report the same salient personality traits. They may use different words to describe these traits, as why should they not, but nonetheless the same ones keep cropping up, no matter what the technique used to uncover them. To use the words most often chosen to describe these traits, they are: egocentricity, low tolerance for tension, dependency, and feeling of or longing for omnipotence.

These are jargon words, and so it will be useful to talk about each of them in more detail.

Egocentricity describes the set of mind in which most of one's concern is with one's own needs and pleasures. The concerns of others are largely a matter of indifference to the egocentric. He seeks the center of the stage; the first person singular pronoun rattles through his speech like drum taps. Psychoanalytically, the term for egocentricity is narcissism, adapted by Freud from the Greek myth of the beautiful youth Narcissus who fell in love with his own reflection in the water (and died, still pining, condemned by the gods for his cruel foolishness in declining to give others his love). We are all more or less narcissistic, in the sense that all of us basically love ourselves more than any other. And there was a time in our lives when this self-love was natural, normal, and necessary: the stage of primary narcissism is placed in early infancy; it coincides with the period during which a baby does not recognize and distinguish himself from the objects or the people offering him gratification; for him, during this period, reality is only the recognition of his need and its gratification. His instinctual impulses are directed solely toward himself.

Low tolerance for tension is the character trait perhaps most often mentioned in connection with alcoholics. Stimulus and reaction are so closely interwoven, with the alcoholic, that they are practically one thing. Resentment, anger, hostility, rage, anxiety, frustration, mild apprehension, or sudden and overwhelming fury—anything that creates tension is the Achilles' heel of the alcoholic. The tension can come from some trivial occurrence of everyday life, or it can well up from some deep-seated psychic conflict, it makes no difference, the alcoholic personality is not gaited to withstand it. He is impatient. He is intolerant of his own moods and those of others. He demands that things go smoothly. If they do not, when they do not, he reacts immediately. His reaction is as swift as that of the baby who awakens hungry, experiencing tension. Like the baby, he is at once caught up in a squall.

Dependency, as a trait, is likewise regressive. There is nothing morally wrong with regression; we all do it: sleep is a kind of regression, a return, however fleeting, to a time when we were fully cared for and protected, and needed not fend for ourselves. No mammal is more helpless than the human during its infancy; and any situation that threatens the individual may well remind him of how, when he was a wholly dependent infant, all was well. The dependent individual will, for unconscious reasons, always seek to be taken care of: he may contrive his marriage to a strong, maternal woman; he may wangle jobs in which he can depend in some way on the one who hired him; in any life situation he may so act as to seem to deserve the care and concern and regard of others.

And finally there is the feeling of omnipotence. This trait, too, is almost universally reported by the psychiatrists and psychologists who have sought to establish *the* alcoholic personality. (Sometimes they call it grandiosity.) We have encountered this concept before, when we were discussing the psychic and unconscious factors that impel us to drink, but in its more pronounced form as an alcoholic trait it demands further discussion.

Why should someone who is quite obviously damaging himself, poisoning the regard of all those around him, undermining health, career, and future—why should someone in such a plight feel omnipotent? How can it be that a man enslaved to a drug addiction can be so blind? And yet it is the case. It has puzzled every therapist in the field. Years ago, Sándor Radó * wrote: "I must admit . . . I could not grasp the economics of this state of mind until a patient himself gave me the explanation. He said: 'I know all the things that people say when they upbraid me. But, mark my words, doctor, *nothing* can happen to *me*.' This, then, is the patient's position. The elation has reactivated his narcissistic belief in his *invulnerability*, and all of his better insight and all of his sense of guilt are shattered on this bulwark."

The same mental attitude was described in the same terms by Harry M. Tiebout,† who wrote: "[It] is . . . difficult to put one's finger on. It may be described as a peculiar unconscious sense of invulnerability. The patients create the impression that the disaster, however threatening, cannot affect them. They are psychically untouched by danger. While consciously troubled, they have a serene unconscious belief in their own survival; they just cannot be licked."

Egocentricity; low tolerance for tension; dependency; and a sense of omnipotence: these four traits share two things in common: each is a vestigial trace of infancy and each is, presuming a relative degree of intensity, neurotic.

* Dr. Radó has been the director of the Psychoanalytic Clinic connected with the Columbia Presbyterian Medical Center. He was (1931–1941) educational director of the New York Psychoanalytical Institute.
† Dr. Tiebout is an analyst with many years of experience in the field of alcoholism. He is vice-chairman of the Connecticut Commission on Alcoholism.

There is in every one of us, without exception, some trace of each of these traits. It is the combination of two or more of them, grossly intensified, that predisposes some of us toward the selection of alcoholism as the particular symptom.

And why toward alcoholism? The point is that for some of us there is the memory, deep in the unconscious, of a magic substance. Magically it relieved tension; magically it restored the feeling of omnipotence; all of us were dependent on it; nor, at that early stage of our existence, were we aware that it was proffered us from without, by someone else. Such a consideration is, to a baby, a quibble. His satisfaction requires of him no gratitude to someone else; he can, if he chooses, regard the magical relief of tension as something that he has himself achieved quite passively: feel need, get satisfaction. Thus the magical substance that came from breast or bottle fed each of the infant's characteristics alike—his egocentricity (or early narcissism), his intolerance for tension, his dependency, and his sense of omnipotence.

Either because his need was too deliciously satisfied or because he fancied it was never satisfied enough, he will forever after retain in his unconscious symbolic goals, impossible of attainment, but inextricably intertwined with the magical substance.

When he was empty and hungry and forlorn and frightened and anxious, the substance (milk) fed him and warmed him and soothed him.

What substance is there, approved and even recommended by society, that will fulfill the same function? Only alcohol. Only alcohol will (always meretriciously, always impossibly) seem to assist in the attainment of the unconscious goals sought by those in whom these four traits flourish like hardy weeds.

There is of course no law that decrees these traits shall be confined to any one given personality type. On the contrary, the laws of probability are overwhelmingly against such a conclusion. For consider: since all four date from early infancy, there will be overlaid upon them the experiences of a consequent childhood, puberty, and adolescence, each experience coloring, affecting, and changing the earliest mental conceptions. The adult personality is the sum of them all.

A myriad experiences and impressions crowd in upon us every day of our lives; chance, wholly capricious, may well determine how we receive them, how we react to them, which of them we receive—in short, which may be meaningful to the ego structure. The infant in whom two or three or four of these four traits will be marked may be an only child, he may be one of twelve; his parents may be poor and obscure, they may be wealthy or celebrated; he may grow up rebellious or conformist, placid or volatile, impetuous or lazy, brilliant or dull. Select your own adjectives, construct your own basic personality: it makes little difference—whatever it be, there is the chance that the constellation of pre-alcoholic traits may figure in it, and may come to grow in intensity so as eventually to overwhelm it.

The possibilities are endless. The infant's mother may have been overly solicitous or insufficiently loving. Especially intolerance to tension can result from a multiplicity of causes: anything that threatens emotional security may turn the trick: rejection, fancied rejection, overprotection, fancied overprotection, parental discord or separation. Moreover, since the trait of egocentricity carries with it the narcissistic need to replenish constantly one's self-esteem, it may result in a rambunctious, aggressive person who seeks the regard of others by force, or in a meek and passive person who attempts to show how he is deserving of regard by shunning conflict and turning to the world only a humble and submissive façade. Indeed, the same individual may do both.

And the many variations possible within these sub-types

must be combined with the many permutations flowing from the threat to the infant's emotional security, with the equally numerous possible configurations of family background, with the truly infinite number of possibilities of stimuli selected for meaningful reception, and (but perhaps by no means finally) with the potential variations within the germ plasm itself. We thus postulate a large number, multiplied by still larger numbers, multiplied in turn by infinity. There can be, in the face of such a purely arithmetical consideration, no astonishment that alcoholics have various different personalities or have achieved different levels of success in life or are overwhelmed by their psychic difficulties at different ages.

In this connection, it cannot be too imperiously urged that the process of alcoholism as a neurotic symptom is dynamic. Nothing could be more erroneous than to visualize the four underlying traits of the pre-alcoholic personality as being always in safe abeyance for most drinkers and always in riotous command over a few others. The factors of life are always in delicate balance. It is not impossible to conceive of an individual whose early life would seem to have predetermined him to alcoholism, but who nevertheless at no time encountered precisely the intricately interwoven set of circumstances that would have proven, for him, fatal. Just so, it is likewise reasonable to suppose that many alcoholics would not be in the grip of their neurosis were it not for some situation that ravaged the strength of their ego structure.

Everything in life is in flux. Change is the only constant. The young man or woman of, say, twenty-two, who today does not let that day go by in which he (or she) orders at least two drinks, may tomorrow be an alcoholic or a teetotaler —and chance will play an important part in the drama.

We have said that the choice of symptom, the nudge in the direction of alcoholism, results from the intensification of two or more of the predisposing pre-alcoholic traits. Now we have added that all is change, that those traits may be in the process of growth or of decline. The question may be fairly put: what will tend to strengthen such traits? and what weaken them?

It is a matter of common observation that many alcoholics come from families in which there is at least one relative who is also an alcoholic. This has, in turn, fostered the notion that alcoholism is hereditary. Something like sixty to seventy per cent of alcoholic patients report near relatives who were alcoholics. It is suggestive. But the evidence, the carefully assayed evidence, indicates that it is an environmental influence, not an inherited taint, that tilts the individual in the direction of alcoholism. Ann Rowe * studied thirty-six children who had been removed from their own homes by court order because of severe alcoholism in one or both parents. The children, when they were placed in foster homes, averaged five-and-one-half years of age. Twenty-seven years later, these children had attained a general adult adjustment and overall personality development comparable to that of the general population. Not one was an alcoholic.

But if heredity is not a factor, certainly environment is, as are also the social pressures to which the individual must adjust. There are some, indeed, who hold that such social pressures may be determinant in causing a neurosis. But it is more likely that the neurosis, the collapse of mental and emotional balances, the subversion in the healthy development of the ego, occurred archaically in the life of the individual, or was at the very least first initiated at that time. The role of social pressures, however, and of environment in general, can by no means be underestimated; what one's father habitually does, or what is socially approved and urged, becomes a component

* Dr. Rowe has been for several years connected with the Department of Applied Physiology of Yale University.

of the superego; and so it is possible that the act of drinking, even the act of drinking to excess habitually, may at the same time bring instinctual gratification and satisfy the superego. And what, after all, is character, if it is not the ego's adjustment to the demands of the external world, the instincts, and the superego?

There are, additionally, exogenous factors that can influence the individual to drink, to drink excessively, and even to drink in the direction of an addiction. Physical pain is one such; alcohol's analgesic property can be exploited to induce, in a theretofore reasonably well adjusted personality, a tendency toward addiction. Remove the external stimulus, end the pain—arthritis, neuritis, whatever it may be—and the mature strength of the ego will once again be sufficient to meet the threat of encroachment by any or all of the predisposing traits.

But the most important factor, the one which is more powerful than any other in strengthening these traits and, indeed, in enabling them to crowd all other traits into the background and completely dominate the personality, is the pharmacological property of the drug itself. The predisposing traits urge the individual to the use of alcohol, alcohol emphasizes and enhances the traits themselves, and so the individual has recurrent recourse to the magical substance. The cycle is now closed, and it is vicious indeed. It is a cyclical regime which, unless it can be interrupted, will lead inexorably to addiction, severe physical and psychical damage, and death.

II

Symptoms take place in people. They can be described in technical or in popular language, but they mean more when we can see them in growth, in people. And so it may be helpful to take a very brief tour through a gallery of quick sketches of some alcoholics. The subjects for these sketches were chosen quite at random; a different group would, while of course having different life stories to offer and probably also different personalities, be from the clinical standpoint not appreciably different from this group.

George K is an investment banker, a handsome and prepossessing man, a man of easy charm and affability. He is conveniently aged for remembering birthdays: his years march with the century: but he looks and acts younger. Encountering him casually, one would conclude only that life had singled K out for particular good fortune.

His good luck, one would think, started early. His father was a man of means, sufficient so that he was able to devote himself to a successful career in public life. In consequence, K, the youngest of six children, saw little of his father who was, when K was born, already in his fifties. K remembers one summer when his parents and older brothers and sisters went to Europe and he was left with servants in the big house in the Berkshires. He remembers how he pretended to be self-sufficient, but how in fact he was frightened and lonely.

K married when he was twenty-four. There is nothing extraordinary about such an event at such an age, but K says today he was too young. It was an alliance that never promised very good results: K had been flattered by the girl's attentions, she was clearly available to be married, he popped the question more because he felt it was expected of him than because he loved her or wanted to marry her. Almost at once he regretted he had done so.

An unhappy marriage gave him, however, a convenient rationalization for his drinking during the late twenties and early thirties. He was on his way up in the financial community, in those Prohibition days. Working for him there was his charm and handsome appearance. K was, moreover, no fool: his intelligence was and is well above the average. He drank often and hard. It was not an unusual thing to do, for a man as well fixed as he was, and in his circle. If, on the other hand, there was no liquor to be had, K did not repine. Today, thinking back, trying to capture the moment in time when drinking first became a problem in his life, K finds that he has a tendency to look for that moment earlier and earlier. Was it when his wife fell sick? Was it when he was still in his twenties? When he was in his teens? He cannot be sure.

Objectively, the trouble started when his wife, diagnosed as psychotic, was taken to a sanitarium. K had mixed emotions about this tragedy: at once he experienced guilt and remorse, but also felt free from obligations which he believed he should never have undertaken. Alone, he began to romp.

For a man with money, good looks, charm, and vitality, New York in the late thirties was a fine place to romp. He squired models to the town's swankier supper clubs. He gave up his Westchester home and moved to a small apartment in town, and still later to a hotel. The change is of some interest. In an apartment, one must take care of oneself. In a hotel, one can be taken care of.

He drank. His business associates could sympathize and say it was because of the tragedy in his life. They urged him to get a divorce and marry again. At length he did but still he drank.

By now the problem bulked big in his life. There were several episodes when he was hospitalized for his steady, excessive drinking; there were as many times when nurses were on twenty-four-hour duty in his apartment, caring for him. He missed Mondays at the office, then Tuesdays. His firm, in which he was a partner, was dissolved for the sole purpose of getting rid of him. Once he thought he would kill himself:

he tried to drown himself in his bathtub. It was more a token gesture of self-pity than a serious attempt at self-destruction, and K knew it, but it was also a reflection of his profound despondency, his dislike for his way of life. Still he drank.

He was fifty when he undertook, at his second wife's extreme urging, to seek help. He debated whether or not he should certify himself for admission into a psychiatric clinic for several months. He shopped around. He tried Antabuse (but experimented with it, to see whether he could not drink while taking the Antabuse). He tried group psychotherapy and was proud that he never missed a meeting of the group (except when he was in the hospital, as a result of one of his frequent slips). He tried individual psychotherapy (but kept right on drinking).

But K was trying, and he was beginning to get a measure of insight into his difficulties. He recalls how one Friday, at the end of his work-week, he planned all day what he would do when he left the office. "I was going to go straight to bed," he said, "and stay there all weekend. As soon as I got inside the door, I was going to head for bed. I could see the whole deal. How Nancy would bring me a bowl of soup. She'd nurse me, feed me, take care of me. That's all I wanted. I wouldn't have anything to worry about. If only I could have had it, just like that. . . ."

But as it happened, he stopped, on the way home, to have a drink with some friends; the next day he had a hangover, and it was a day of frustration, too; his apartment was being painted and he had to decamp with his wife to a hotel. He took a bottle with him; the next six days were blank; and then he was once again in a hospital.

It is at times like this that we rack our brains: How could K do such a thing? Why did he do it? Didn't he understand? Can half a century of experience teach a man nothing? Doesn't he know he shouldn't? His wife and the senior partner of his firm—they both knew K to be an able, intelligent, resourceful person, they had seen these qualities in him at home and at the office. Why? they demand. What is the matter with him?

It may help, in order to understand K's behavior, to forget him for a moment and think of two other people, neither of them alcoholics, although one is a morphine addict and the other well may be a drug addict by now, for he had the fateful traits to a marked degree.

Let us take him first. He was seen at Elmira, in the New York State Reformatory, when he made a routine appearance before the State Parole Commission. He was a youth of about nineteen. It was his second hitch at Elmira; he had been lagged for violating parole. It is the circumstances of this violation that are of interest: He had got hold of a gun (violation) and, out on the streets after midnight (violation), had held up a citizen (violation) and taken from him his watch (violation). Any one of these four violations would have been enough, presuming it would be detected, to send him back to Elmira, but he made sure by involving himself in four. And he went further: he violated, as well, the simplest dictates of logic. For of course it is quite possible for a parolee to violate his parole without being detected; one must presume that every hour of every day is marked, somewhere, by such violations, unknown to the authorities. But what this youngster did was to hold up and rob a man whom he knew, and who, he knew, knew him. He must have known, as he jabbed the gun in his acquaintance's ribs, that it would be only a matter of minutes before his parole officer would be given the word to pick him up.

He was back in Elmira the next day.

One of the commissioners was asked to explain the youngster's apparently insane behavior.

The commissioner shrugged. "I guess he just can't stand

93

freedom," he said. "Unconsciously, he insists on being taken care of."

And now the other man. This other is a doctor of medicine. As sometimes happens with doctors, to whom drugs are available, he became addicted to morphine. He went to the Public Health Service Hospital at Lexington, Kentucky, where he was treated for his addiction, and whence he was at length discharged to try to piece together the shards of his career. He was an extremely able physician, a brilliant diagnostician and exceptionally well fitted to work with patients. And so it happened that, despite the history of his addiction, he was given a berth on the staff of a small hospital.

One day, the charge nurse being momentarily and wrongfully absent from her post, the doctor noticed that the safe in which were kept the hospital's stores of narcotic drugs was not locked. He slipped swiftly into the post, his hand darted into the safe—and came away with a fistful of Demerol ampules. It cannot be argued that the doctor was unaware that such stores are checked: he knew they are always and routinely checked. It cannot be argued that he thought he would not be suspected: he was the first candidate for suspicion. It cannot be argued that he hoped he would not be questioned and at length dismissed. And yet he stole the narcotic. What went through his mind, in the split second when his hand was inside the safe? Did he think of the years of training that had gone into making him a doctor? Did he think about the career, soon to go on the rocks? And if he thought of none of these things, *why* didn't he?

It must be supposed that he did think of these things, and probably of still other considerations, all of them grave deterrents to his action. And yet, when his hand came out of the safe, it held the Demerol. There is only one conclusion: the unconscious (and unattainable) symbol which he sought, and which was for him represented by the ampules, was a more powerful consideration than any other, and overwhelmed any and all others. He was bidden by his unconscious to do what he did, and such was the strength of this unconscious demand as to negate all logic.

Ask that doctor: "Doctor, would you wilfully do something that would smash your career?" and his answer would of course be an unhesitating "No," probably accompanied by a frown of curiosity as to why his questioner would dream of putting such a silly proposition to him.

Ask the youngster in Elmira: "Which would you rather: be free, outside these walls, or be jailed here for two years?" and he would think his questioner crazy.

And K—ask K, on that Friday afternoon: "K, which do you want: to go home and go to bed and be taken care of by your wife? Or do you want to start out on a drunk that will land you in the disturbed ward of a hospital a week hence?"

Logic, the conscious system of the mind, the sensible considerations and reflections of healthy mentality—these things are swept away like chips of wood on the ungovernable storm waves of the mind's unconscious system.

And K ended up in a disturbed ward, with wooden panels on either side of his bed.

His day-nurse tried to sell him on the notion of joining Alcoholics Anonymous. "You really ought to," she told him. She was, of course, not the first. He told her to keep her nose out of his business.

He had, at one point or another, gone to four different doctors in the course of his treatment up till then. He was, for one reason or another, angry with them all. Now a fifth doctor entered the picture.

He asked K: "Can you go two or three months without liquor?"

"Sure," said K.

"Can you go one month without?"

"Sure," said K, with perhaps a shade less conviction.

"You'll have resistance, to giving it up," the doctor pursued. "What will you do, if the urge is great?"

K did not answer.

"Are you a spiritual man?" the doctor asked.

K thought. He had gone to a Presbyterian Sunday School as a boy. He was a member of no church now. He did not consider himself an agnostic, however, nor an atheist; he was not, to use his own phrase, smart-alecky about religion.

"I wish," said the doctor, "that you would try Alcoholics Anonymous."

There was a pause. K found himself wishing that the doctor had said: "You *ought* to try A.A." Then it would have been easy for him to jeer and refuse.

That Monday night he went to his first A.A. meeting. Thereafter, for nearly three months, he attended A.A. meetings in one or another part of New York at least three nights a week. But truth to tell, he did not much like it. At the same time, he did. He wasn't sure. Then one night he ran into an old friend, a pal of his days in the speakeasies and his nights in the supper clubs. This man asked K where he had been keeping himself. K was a trifle irritated by the remark: there seemed to him to be a little condescension in the tone.

"I've been going to A.A. meetings," he said stiffly.

His friend's jaw dropped, and an incredulous look spread over his face.

"I think I'm hooked," K heard himself say. "I think I'm an alcoholic, and I think I want to belong to A.A." But at that moment he did not really think he was an alcoholic; at that moment he did not think he was hooked; at that moment, he told himself with a touch of panic, he was not even sure he wanted to join A.A. As it happened, his future teetered on the reaction of an unstable friend. This man, wholly unwittingly, did K a tremendous favor.

"You're off your rocker," he said, roughly. "What the hell's the matter with you, anyway? Are you kidding?"

That night K attended another A.A. meeting, and the next day he began systematically to take each of the Twelve Steps.* He has not had a drink since. Because he was and is a man of obvious ability, with very real qualities of leadership, K rose rapidly in the fellowship of A.A. and has for some time been the chairman of his A.A. group. Because he has taken his responsibilities seriously, K has had increasing insights into his own problems. He is aware, for example, of his dependency pattern; increasingly conscious of how, in fighting his dependency, in pretending to be independent, he was in fact being merely defiant. When someone said to K: "You should!" he reacted angrily and stubbornly; he did the opposite: he was showing, he thought, his independence. "Don't!" they told him; so he did. "Do!" they ordered him; so he refused. "Please," said someone, finally, "I wish you would"; and he was baffled. There was no opportunity for him to show how "independent" he was.

And this crux in his life was capped by another, the moment when, K being still uncertain about his course, a friend and companion of many years' standing bade him, in effect, "Don't!" So, promptly, he did, and has forever since been the better for it, especially inasmuch as he now understands why.

K's parents were, in relation to him, older than parents usually are, and more detached and less concerned; K's de-

---

* This phrase is anticipatory. The Twelve Steps constitute the cardinal programmatic aspect of Alcoholics Anonymous, than which, for alcoholics, there is no better therapeutic approach. The role of this lay organization, which has done so much to show doctors how alcoholics can be recovered, will be discussed later in this book.

97

pendency pattern, then, was the result of his unconscious striving for something of which he felt he had been cheated. He wanted someone to take care of him as he had never been taken care of; it was his unconscious symbolic goal.

Richard W, on the other hand, was an only child of young parents who gave him everything, protected him from everything, and were in every way too solicitous and too provident —at least for W. Over three generations the W family had built up a prosperous commercial enterprise in a southern city; from the day of his birth, W was regarded as the heir apparent to the business. He would never need to struggle. He had as a boy, in addition to a mother and father, a nursemaid, a governess, and later a tutor. When he married, W tried to make sure, unconsciously, that his wife would be the kind of person from whom he would always be able to get more of the same.

He makes constant demands on her time and her attention and her care. He claims he cannot fall asleep at night unless she reads to him aloud. He wants her with him always. If she leaves him for so much as a trip to the hairdresser's, he is devastated and must have recourse to the bottle.

Unlike K, W has at present very limited insight into his characteristic dependency pattern. Unlike K, W still drinks. And all the advantages that were his at his birth may do him no good. He recognizes he has a drinking problem but refuses to recognize that this problem is only a symptom of a more serious emotional disorder. He may change his mind, he may not. So far, he clings to his notion of independence: defiance of anyone who would gainsay his infantile wishes. It is one of his wishes that his problem with alcohol be considered as something wholly separate from his mental life; analogous, shall we say, to a wen, or a birthmark; something that can easily be removed with a nick of the surgeon's knife. Why is the surgeon so obstinate? Why does he refuse W this simple service—W, for whom life has been a succession of services smoothly performed? To tell W that the case is not so simple is to thwart him. Thwarted, he feels tension, and becomes apprehensive. Apprehensive, he storms into a rage. Raging, he reacts. His reaction is quite unconsciously motivated and flies in the face of the resolution he made only yesterday, or maybe only an hour ago, that he will never drink again. The rhythm of his impulsive reaction was established in the first weeks of his life: hunger-tension requires satiety-relaxation. The bottle he reaches for ("No! Don't, Dick!" "Ah, go to hell!") is the bottle of his infancy. Then he was urged to empty it. Now he needs no urging.

The swift course of W's impulsive reaction calls to mind another alcoholic, Joe S. He was raised far on the other side of those symbolic railroad tracks from either K or W, but he has as much physical good looks and charm as either of them. S is the son of immigrant parents; he is of the working class; most of his adult life he has been a machinist or a construction boss; meeting him today the impression one gets is of a likeable, articulate, intelligent man, a man who, clad in the appropriate clothes, would fit easily and mix comfortably in any social circle. His doctor's first impression was rather different.

She saw a man in his early thirties, a man spitting mad and bitterly resentful, scarcely able to talk. He was in her office not from choice but because he had been sent there by New York City's Home Term Court. He was there alone, but the hand of the law had metaphorically pointed his way and gripped his elbow. In his first interview he could only complain bitterly, abuse, scold, and reproach any and everyone who had a hand in his being there.

His wife—it was her fault! No—it was his sister-in-law's

fault! And that crumby judge down at that curseword court! When he could spare time to do so, S railed at the doctor as well. What the hell did she think she could do for him? Why had he been sent to a clinic for alcoholics in the first place? Why should that dopey curseword judge think he was an alcoholic, for curseword's sake? But S was required to come, and to come back.

At his second interview, the doctor learned more about him, and so did the psychologist attached to the clinic. "You know," S told the doctor, "I work as a construction boss for the XX Company, but what I really am is, I'm a painter."

In her experience, the doctor had met many alcoholics who, to shore up their bankrupt self-esteem, would lie grandly about their social background or their talents. But she sensed that this was no random boast. She asked him to bring some examples of his work to the clinic. He did. S worked in abstract designs, with a brilliant palette and a sure sense of form. He left ten or a dozen paintings in the doctor's office, and with time most of them were sold to other patients or to other doctors.

S agreed to enter group psychotherapy. Actually, he had no choice: he was bound by court order to follow the doctor's suggestions. But by no means did he think he was sick. He refused to grant that he was an alcoholic or indeed that alcohol caused him any particular problem. Sure, he went on an occasional toot—maybe once a month or so, for two or three days. But remorse? "I put on a clean shirt, wash my face, and forget it." The doctor knew better. She had talked to his wife.

Out of his many sessions in group therapy, twice a week over a period of several months, a picture of S emerged. It was a picture of an impulsive man, trigger-tempered and itchy-footed, a man for whom stimulus and reaction were so closely interwoven as to be one and the same thing. He had often been told, in his thirty-odd years, that it might be a good idea for him to pause and reflect before acting. But S had seldom looked and often leaped.

Bored with school, the lesson he best learned was how to play hookey. Irritated at home by his father's nagging, he took off for the Great Lakes and got a job on a tugboat. Chafing under that life, he shipped aboard a Danish freighter bound for South America. He couldn't wait to get back and get ashore. Back home, he met a girl ("I always knew the size, it was only a matter of picking the color and shape") and married her. He was soon sorry, but she was sorrier sooner; anything that provoked him was her fault, and she was to feel too often the sting of his tongue and of his fist. On such occasions, he was usually drunk.

When war was declared, S enlisted. He was glad of the excuse to leave home. He had wanted to join the Marines ("They had the best uniform"), but settled on the Seabees when he found they would give him a rating. In service, S drank more than ever ("The Navy was stuck with you. They couldn't fire you. They could kill you but they couldn't eat you.") Throughout his service, S courted danger and volunteered for hazardous work. He was convinced that nothing could happen to hurt him. He was an inveterate gambler, with dice and with his life. And he drank. If he was feeling good, he drank "to exhilarate that feeling." If he was feeling despondent—and his mood swings were rapid and wide—he drank "to pull out of it." He drank anything and everything, including a potent concoction they called cane squeezings: "Three or four drinks, and you'd spin around like a dog chasing his damn tail."

So long as he was in the service, somebody else had to worry, somebody else was responsible, somebody else was making the decisions. The money was regular, the drinking was easy—S even managed to do a snow job on one of his officers and wangle his whisky ration from him—and the pressure was off. Then they put him on a boat and sent him home. "It took fifteen days," S has said, "but it seemed like fifteen minutes."

Home, S got a divorce, a job, and a new wife. His job was as a trouble-shooter on construction projects for a company with installations scattered all over the country, and it kept him on the move. His wife, whom he had met at an art exhibit, knew about his hot temper and his drinking problem before she married him, but did so nevertheless. She moved about the country with him. She tried not to object to his habit of packing a pint of whisky on his hip when he started off in the morning to work; she tried not to seem to interfere when he began missing Mondays from work, and then occasional Tuesdays as well; she kept her mouth shut when he was arrested for driving a car while drunk and had to pay a $600 bribe to keep his name off the police blotter and his license in his wallet; but the strain grew greater when his drinking finally resulted in his being fired.

S had been doing work generally assigned to graduate engineers, but he had not graduated even from high school. He found it impossible to land another job as good. He pretended not to care; he pretended he had always wanted to paint in any event. And his drinking increased. His second wife, as had his first before her, learned how it felt to be slugged by her husband.

Then one night they were invited to a party at the apartment of her married sister. Of course there were drinks, quite naturally. And of course, quite naturally, something happened to make S lose his temper. Today, when he tries to recall what triggered the incident, S cannot. All that he can remember is that it was something "unimportant. I think someone said something, passed some remark, maybe a dirty crack. I don't know. If it had been anything important, I'd be able to remember it. Believe me, it was nothing."

But it was enough to make him kick a coffee table into smithereens and plunge out into the night to wander from saloon to saloon, building up a package of alcohol and resentment and hostility until at length he returned, socked his wife, and ended up in jail. It was a few morning's later that he came to the doctor's office, still caught up in his infantile rage.

It was this hostile, fractious, stubborn, and unrepentant man who sat suspiciously in group psychotherapy sessions, back in the early spring of 1950. Something began to happen to him. He still believed that he himself was attending these sessions only because a judge had ordered him to, not because there was any personal need for therapy, but he began to perceive how alcohol could cause problems for other people. From recognizing the neurotic pattern in others to wondering about himself was not a very difficult step for S to take. He listened to the others talking about their early childhoods; inside him, memories stirred.

During these weeks, S was not touching a drop (he was taking Antabuse; one of the earliest patients to take the drug, he had been given some alcohol on top of a dose so that he would learn with immediate impact the dangers of drinking; "I could *feel* the red come up," he said later, "and my heart beating like a bullfrog, and my ears ringing"). But those dry days were not easy either for him or for his wife. She would wake him when the alarm clock went off; he would smash the clock and turn on her to smash her as well. Once she had to run away from him, run at night through the woods near their home to the highway where she could catch a bus to New York and seek refuge in the doctor's home overnight. In those difficult days, S was depressed, impatient, intolerant, irritable, jittery—

in precisely the mood he was accustomed to alleviating by having a quick drink.

But something had indeed happened. He had seen, from the experience of his companions in the group therapy sessions, what might well happen to him if he were to relax his resolve for an instant. He hung on, by his nails.

He had, fortunately, more than merely resolution. He had as well a growing insight into his own conflicts, into the battle that was raging within him. He could never have learned to stop drinking by a simple act of will: he had in addition to learn *why* he had done so thoughtlessly and so impulsively the things that he had hated himself for next morning. He had in addition to learn *why* he found it necessary to drink. Once that lesson was well learned, his ego would be strong enough to resist and repel the gnawing temptations, goading, prodding, eternally creating excuses for him, the terrifyingly powerful impulses that came from his unconscious and threatened to engulf him and destroy the patient, careful progress of months.

A battle of this kind, while it is grindingly exhausting to the individual whose mind and central nervous system are the battleground, can be enormously exciting and even inspiring to the beholder. The beholder, if he be the psychiatrist, is of course never passive; on the contrary, as best he can he is constantly working to analyze the unconscious forces, help the ego to gather its strength, forewarn against possible pitfalls, and assist in bringing to consciousness the repressed wishes, hostilities, and other instinctual strivings which are at the core of the difficulty. There are times, too, when the tension of the battle is relieved by the unexpected, and the beholder, at least, can relax and smile, reassured that one skirmish in the battle has gone well. Such a moment arose, in S's battle, when he had been in group therapy for perhaps eight months.

S and his wife had been married for about two years. She

wanted children but he—he was a child himself. Did he want a baby crowding into his world, a baby that would compete with him for the attention of his wife, and compete probably all too successfully? The therapist in charge of the group judged, on the basis of his observation of S, that the time was perhaps not the most propitious for S and his wife to have a baby; that the additional strain on S's mental economy might prove too great; that the frustrations he would experience, in attempting to rival a baby for his wife's regard, were too likely to drive him once again to drink. So persuaded was the therapist, indeed, that, when S announced to the group his intention to father a baby, the therapist undertook to talk to Mrs. S and warn her against such a step at that time.

S and his wife were both furious. They appealed over the therapist's head to the doctor. The doctor of course felt that the therapist had been unwise, but she was struck by something else. She could not help noticing how S, as he made his appeal, was behaving quite like a small boy who, ordered to do something unpleasant by his father, promptly importunes his mother for redress of grievances. Moreover, it was not enough for S that the doctor should overrule the therapist, that Mother should overrule Father; S wanted to make sure that Father realized he was all alone in being wrong. He wanted all his brothers and sisters to side with him as well. And so he referred the question to the group.

A week or so later, he burst into the doctor's office, his face radiant. "It's all settled!" he cried. "The group says I can have a baby!"

In fact, some six years after his first appearance in the doctor's office, S and his wife have three children, and S has never since had recourse to the magic substance of alcohol to assuage the temper and the impatience and the irritability that formerly ruled his life. Only twice in that period, indeed, has he been sorely tempted. On each occasion he was temporarily away from his wife. Once, in Panama, far from authority or discipline, secure in the delusion that no one would ever know, prey to a momentary tension, he almost leaped. But this time his ego strength was such that first he looked. He looked back. What he saw was the moment when he was dolefully paying out $600 in bribes to hang on to his job and his driver's license. He thought to himself: "It can happen again," and "Brandy is cheap, down here in Panama, but $600 is a hell of a price to pay for a drunk." The second time, he was in Florida with his brother-in-law. He went with this man while he got "stinking, crawling drunk. And all the time I wanted to get down there with him. And all the time I was giving myself the horselaugh for wanting to."

S can count himself a lucky man. To be sure, he is not wholly well. He needs more psychotherapy, and knows it. He could profit from psychoanalysis, and knows it—but cannot afford it. But his alcoholism was arrested before the symptom had been transformed into a raging disease. His scrapes with society were minor. His conflicts with those near and dear to him were painful but not mortal. He never, to use a phrase commonly associated with alcoholics, hit bottom, although he brushed up against it once or twice. For him, at one time, there was an inexorable simultaneity of affecting stimulus and reactive explosion, but he has been able to pry the two apart. He can see daylight between them, enough daylight to afford himself time for reflection. He has broken the cycle. In that chink of daylight, there is room for logic to squeeze through, and counsel him, and slow him down, and stop him. Stop him not dead, but alive.

Those in search of a common personality for all alcoholics would despair if they were to meet Frederick G at the interview next after meeting Joe S. Here, they would say, are two nearly diametrically opposite personalities. Where S is rash, G is cautious. S has gambled all his life, G never. S will try anything new, in fact looks for new experiences, new places to be, new acquaintances; G is conservative, sedentary, conformist. S takes a delight in attending group psychotherapy sessions where all the others are upper-middle-class and arriving in his work-clothes, heavy boots, corduroys, plaid shirts; G dresses in the uniform of his kind, quiet cheviots and worsteds Monday-through-Friday, gray flannels and tweed jacket on Saturday, sober serge on Sunday. S has the perverse snobbism that leads him to use colorful slang in polite circles, but G chooses his words slowly and carefully and, above all, circumspectly.

There are some biographical similarities, but they do not convince. Each is about the same age. Each has a sister, in each case two years younger. The mother of each died when he was still a child. Neither was born into affluent circumstances. Each (we can pursue this) is fair-haired, male, and alcoholic (but there is no point in pursuing it).

The similarities that do convince are the presence, to a striking degree, of oral traits in each: intolerance of tension and egocentricity are the most marked. If, in either case, the cyclical disposition toward addiction had become more pronounced, there can be no doubt that the other two traits, in S's case the feeling of omnipotence and in G's a dependency, would have grown to overwhelming proportions. S would have progressed from one rash act to another; G would have become even more the unmanageable infant, constantly seeking a nurse or mother. And the one trend is, after all, only the reverse of the other: dependency is rashness transposed: neither is, in the true sense, independence.

These two quite different men are, then, curiously like.

G first tasted an alcoholic beverage in his late teens. The

beverage was beer, and he was working for an advertising agency as an office boy. The agency was one of those that followed the practice of hiring office boys for the specific purpose of promoting them; they were called C.B.O.B.'s (college-boy office boys), although some of them, and G was one, had gone no further than high school. They ganged together after office hours, these youngsters, and their socially accepted habits were those of the oldest and most experienced. They used to lunch together at the same Third Avenue saloon in New York; and on weekends they would go together to listen to the same hot jazz orchestras. G didn't like beer; he didn't like ale; he liked gin and whisky even less; but he drank, or tried to, drink for drink along with the others, to conform, to be part of the group.

Personable and intelligent, G was promoted fairly fast. His agency sent him to St. Louis to do promotion and media work on a medium-sized account; he shared a house with two other advertising men, and shared too in their country-club life. He began to notice (this was in 1938 and 1939) that his hangovers were always more virulent than those of the others, and he wondered why.

During his hitch in the Navy his drinking was sporadic but intensive. He pulled a lot of sea-duty; whenever he hit the beach, he tried to make up for lost time. Always he tried to learn to drink like a gentleman: here was the goal: college men learned to drink like gentlemen, Navy officers drank like gentlemen (sometimes), and G wanted to be one of them. He did not always succeed. His tolerance for alcohol was never on a par with that of his companions. But he kept trying.

After the war, back again with the agency, he was assigned to a radio program that toured the country, originating from various different cities. Wherever he went he found that his job involved a lot of drinking: he had been told he should entertain the local station bigwigs and was given a liberal expense account to do so, but the local station bigwigs had their own liberal expense accounts with which to entertain him. In one city after another, one night after another, G tried hard to drink, drink for drink, with men to whom hard drinking came easy. It was a matter of pride with G, and at the same time he imagined that it was a matter of good business. When the glasses began to empty, he felt that it was his responsibility to refill them—and he hoped always that the word would get back to New York that he, G, was a good fellow, a good two-fisted drinker, a sharp man in a business deal, but you could never get him drunk, he always had the agency's best interests at heart. Glumly he shot craps with station representatives from New York to Los Angeles. It was a duty. He was delighted, secretly, when the sponsor cancelled the show and he could return to New York to what he conceived would be peace.

But back in New York there was, he found, no hiding place: his department head was himself on the way to addictive drinking and used to ask G to join him in any of the several saloons within walking distance of the office at ten-thirty in the morning (or at ten, or even at nine-thirty). "It would have been," G has said delicately, "unpleasant for me to refuse." Now, to add to his shattering hangovers, G discovered the morning hair-of-the-dog, and now too he began to experience the unpleasant business of what alcoholics call blackouts—periods when he would be unable to remember what had happened, what he had said or done; what some people call *pulling a blank*.

G tried going on the wagon. It was unavailing. He tried limiting the hours of his drinking: "No more ale in the morning" or "No highballs after dinner." That didn't work either. He decided it would be the better part of valor to switch jobs

—and maybe, too, that was all he needed, to get away from his alcoholic boss. He took a job as account executive with a smaller agency. Now he was more his own master: there was no one to watch his comings and goings; his only responsibility was to service what had been a smooth-running account. He formed the habit of dropping in, early every afternoon, to the same Third Avenue saloon where, he knew, he would find a group of congenial regulars, men like himself in the advertising business. With them he drank one ale after another.

It has been said that one cannot get drunk on beer or ale. The brewers have published a number of pamphlets to this effect, and there are physiologists of sound reputation who back them up. So far as G is concerned, they can tell it to Sweeney.

But he did not rely on malt beverages. At home, he would, on an ordinary evening, polish off half of a fifth of gin. If he was more than usually apprehensive he would drink more. His wife (G was married in 1940; there are two children) for a time thought it would be best to drink with him, and in consequence dinner would be served maybe at eight, maybe at eight-thirty, maybe at nine-thirty. She stopped, and began to urge him to stop too. If he had no other reason, she pointed out, there was the drain on their budget, for three or four fifths of gin or whisky in a week can eat a big hole in the paycheck. But G realized there were other reasons. He was beginning to fear that maybe he was addicted to alcohol.

At first he never discussed his fear with anyone. But secretly he went to New York's big Public Library and looked up some books on alcoholism. There was one by a doctor who contended alcoholism is the result of a vitamin deficiency: massive doses of vitamins would, it was argued in this book, successfully combat the physiological dysfunction that resulted in alcoholism. G wrote to the author, asking for the name of a New York physician familiar with his course of treatment.

He was referred to a doctor who followed the prescribed regime, at the same time telling G flatly that he should never drink again. G listened, went away, and drank.

He drank now, and harder, out of a growing sense of inadequacy. His account, which had practically taken care of itself in the past, had suddenly become a problem. The client had doubled his advertising budget to launch a new product, and G got the notion that he was being tested: the way he handled this big new campaign would determine whether he was able to stay in the saddle or not. The increased responsibility led him to drink more often; the increased drink sapped his self-esteem; he began to pity himself and his plight; more anxious than ever, he drank more than ever, and there were now occasions when he would be off on a bat for a couple of days at a time, waking up in strange apartments physically sick and racked by remorse. "Remorse," G has since said, ruefully, "I had the greatest remorses the world has ever seen. I was a really miserable son-of-a-bitch."

Then he was fired. He was not told that it was because of his drinking, it was not necessary to tell him. During the next six months, when he was around looking for a job, he was able to form his own conclusions. Friends of long standing developed suddenly a habit of being away from their desks when he phoned them and of being too busy to return his calls. It had to be because of his drinking, he told himself. But didn't everybody in this business drink? What was so special about him? At length a personnel manager, a man who was a comparative stranger to him, spoke bluntly: "You can't handle it," this man said, not "You drink too much," but "You can't hold it." And the overtones of his remark were: "You can't drink like a gentleman."

To G such a rebuff was more humiliating than to have been told simply, "You can't drink." He bathed himself in self-pity and he lashed himself with self-reproach. This was the time when he decided that he had always been essentially a creative person. No wonder he drank: it was because he had always hated being a huckster. This was an "If only . . ." time: "If only I had gotten straightened out when I was still a kid" and "If only I had stuck to being a writer" and "If only, when I got back to New York, I hadn't found myself working for an alcoholic. . . ."

Self-pity and self-reproach are important emotions to someone carrying on an unhappy love affair with himself. As is the case in every such ill-starred romance, G gradually withdrew from the world; lost interest in everything except himself and his own brooding preoccupations; and came, finally, almost to the point where he would sit, petulant and sulky, licking his wounds, and waiting for something magical to happen that would be the answer to all his problems.

But he did not quite reach that point.

He was fortunate that he did not. We have pointed out that more than anything else the steady, addictive use of alcohol tends to enhance the predisposing traits of the alcoholic personality, and this was the case with G. Moreover, he was unemployed, which meant that there were no routines for him to follow, no disciplines or distractions to disturb the vacuum of his days. Unless something had happened to jolt him out of his growing egocentricity, there can be no question that he would have proceeded into what Dr. Radó has called the pharmacothymic regime, in which alcohol induces a transitory elation, inevitably followed by depression, remorse, and self-reproach, but accompanied also by "the enticing memory of the elation," and a consequent craving for that elation. "This regime is interested in only one problem: depression, and in only one method of attacking it: the administration of the drug."

One after another those who have specialized in the treatment of this neurosis offer testimony as to the dynamic nature of these dominating traits. Indeed, Dr. Tiebout defines addiction as "the slow altering of the personality in the direction of egocentricity." The seeds of this egocentricity are, he agrees, deep within each of us "and, under the nurturing of alcohol, like weeds in a garden, they sprout vigorously and soon overwhelm the other characteristics, so that at last all the gardens look pretty much alike."

But two things were to happen to G that would jolt him out of his regressive drive toward egocentricity. In the first place, he got a job. In the second, like a drowning man clutching at straws, he made a next-to-last desperate attempt to get medical help.

Neither would have succeeded by itself. The job he hated. He regarded it as a comedown. It offered him no opportunity for the creative expression he felt he was capable of. It was personnel work, routine, dull, undemanding. Even as a huckster he had been able to console himself with the notion that his work was glamorous, enviable, and that in that work he was destined for great things. There could be no such delusion in his new job.

The scaling down of values, the setting of sights on more modest goals, is something that many and many an alcoholic has had to achieve. It is part of the chastening process by which he progresses from infantile grandiosity to a realistic regime. A musician now in his forties used, while he was drinking, to claim that there was nothing too difficult for him; he had been a composer as a youngster, had composed three symphonies by the time he was sixteen; when he had difficulty in getting them played, he turned to a career as a concert artist, wholly convinced that he would be at the top of the heap in four or five years. Even as a tormented alcoholic, playing dance music in a dreary little orchestra in a small roadhouse, he remained persuaded of his essential greatness. His sobriety, his mastery of his neurotic symptom, coincided with his realization that there was nothing so terribly tragic about the fact that he had never set the Thames on fire, nor ever would. Another recovered alcoholic, a shipyard worker, now says: "I no longer expect to knock the world dead. I don't need the spectacular. I go to work in the morning, and I come back home at night. I got something else now: a little sense of security—and it's a damn good feeling."

In G's case, typically, such a realistic reevaluation was by no means achieved overnight. In his new job, which he considered demeaning, he continued to drink. The despair hit him when he began to suspect that his new employers knew how much time he was spending in a nearby saloon. The fear was not enough to keep him from drinking in the saloon (at that point there was nothing in heaven or earth that could have stopped him from that), but it was enough to drive him to a newly opened clinic for alcoholics in a city hospital.

He showed up sober. That meant that he would not be at once put to bed in the hospital's in-patient alcoholic ward. Instead he was turned over to a psychiatric social service worker, interviewed, and told to come back for his first counseling appointment the following week. When he did so (for he was badly scared) he met first with a physician who asked him why he was there.

"Because I drink," said G.

"Why don't you stop?" the doctor asked.

It was a good question and maybe, after a year of psychotherapy, it might have even been a fair question. As it was, G only stared stonily at the doctor, hating him, feeling the rage mount inside him.

"Well," said the doctor easily, "we'll see what we can do."

But in two months of interviews with the psychiatric social service worker to whom G had been assigned, the clinic was able to do nothing for him. He continued to drink.

His tolerance for alcohol had never been very high. Even when he was in the Navy and drinking fairly hard during his occasional liberties ashore, G had not been able to pack it away as had his companions. Now at about this time he noticed that his tolerance took a swift nosedive. Now he would be drunk on three or four drinks. And he was encompassed by the dreadful feeling that he had no will. No matter how often or how firmly he resolved, he simply was not able to stop drinking. "I was lost," G has since said. "What are you going to think about yourself, when you find that you *simply have got to drink*, within the hour of your swearing to yourself and your wife that you won't? I'd tell her: Okay, no drinks after dinner. Could I blame her when she got sore, seeing me pour myself a slug, trying to hide it, claiming it was just a nightcap? What the hell was happening to me? *I* didn't know."

One night he made a date to meet his wife, after work. She was to pick him up at a bar near his office. She was a few minutes late—time enough for him to have two drinks. When she arrived, he was still sober. They decided to have a drink or two together, sitting there at the bar, and then go home. G had two more drinks. Waiters had to carry him to a taxicab.

At home, his wife appealed to a doctor who was a family friend. He urged that G go to a specialist in alcoholism who would prescribe Antabuse—something that G had asked for elsewhere but, curiously, never been given.

From the age of eighteen, G had never been able to go more than three weeks without a drink. Alcoholics Anonymous had been of no help to him. A psychiatric social service worker had not succeeded. Massive doses of vitamins had succeeded only in filling him with massive doses of vitamins. He wanted Antabuse. He was given some.

He has not had a drink since.

G says: "It kept me from drinking until I had a chance to straighten myself out. I had tried by myself, with A.A., with self-discipline . . . it gave me the boost I needed."

G entered group psychotherapy, as soon as he started using Antabuse. "I wanted that too," G has said. "I still didn't know why alcohol had affected me the way it did. The group therapy? Well. It wasn't a complete waste of time. But it was the Antabuse that did the trick. It prevented me from making any slips. I take it in the morning, while I am still full of good resolves. And since I've taken it, that's it.

"I was fouled up in my thinking. Antabuse helped me stay on the wagon long enough so that I could get straightened out."

G was in group psychotherapy for more than a year. It is his privilege to speak of it slightingly, but the fact is that it was during that year that he learned *why* he had found it necessary to drink. A year after quitting the group, he was still taking Antabuse regularly, every morning. He was asked when he would stop.

"It's like brushing my teeth," he said. "Why should I stop? I don't need it any more, at least I don't think I do, but why should I stop?"

The particular method that was helpful for G might well not be helpful to the next alcoholic. And it is, in any event, not so important as what has happened to him since. There has been, for G, a revival of all the interests he had and shared with his wife before the symptom of his neurosis cast its shadow over him: he spends time at home now, reading; he goes to the ballet and to the opera; a whole world is opening up before him again. If he has a complaint, it is that his drinking friends seem to him so dull—and so, rather than spend time with them, he prefers to do something that he knows in advance will be more rewarding. Outward he has turned his interests, outward to the world: he is active in the social-action group of his Protestant church, working with Puerto Rican children, helping them to find their places in their new land.

"When I think," he has said, "of the hours I used to waste—well, maybe *waste* isn't the right word. Maybe I had to learn, and maybe that was the way I had to take. But now! Now I feel like a reformer!"

But G is no reformer, and never will be. What has happened to G is this: he has learned a maturing lesson—that to invest emotion and interest and regard in other people is a healthy way to live.

Which is to say, G is, belatedly, becoming an adult emotionally.

So far, the only subjects that have sat for these quick and impressionist sketches of alcoholics are men. To be sure, most American alcoholics *are* men, but the only moral that can be drawn from this statement is a sociological one: the custom of drinking, among us, is wider-spread, as we have seen, among men than among women and the social sanctions more permissive for men than for women. How closely custom and tradition influence differing rates of alcoholism on the basis of sex can best be appreciated by reference to some comparative studies made a few years ago of the ratios between men and women alcoholics in various countries. In England, where women, at least among the poor, drink without condemnation in the pubs along with the men, the ratio is one woman to two men; in the United States it was, at least until recently, 1 to 6; in Switzerland it was 1 to 12; in Norway it was 1 to 23. Now that drinking by women has become far more socially acceptable, as has been the case in the United States in recent years, we must expect that the ratio will level off. Indeed, it seems already to have tended in this direction, if the present case-load of clinicians specializing in the problems of alcoholism is any test.

Sometimes women alcoholics are launched toward addictive drinking by the practice of keeping their excessively drinking husbands company. Sometimes they begin by getting into the habit of drinking to combat the pain of their menses or to alleviate pre-menstrual tension. Sometimes—but men, too, begin their drinking for different conscious reasons and end by drinking excessively for different reasons, and there does not seem to be any particular set of circumstances that sets off the woman alcoholic from the man alcoholic. Certainly it is necessary that she have the same constellation of predisposing personality traits. The likelihood is that she comes by these traits in much the same way as does her brother or her husband or her lover, or as did her father, or as may her son.

Social disapproval does, however, lead to an important difference in the drinking habits of the woman alcoholic. Because only in a very tolerant social milieu may women drink like men, there is among women alcoholics far more solitary drinking. Indeed, the suspicion grows that there are more secret women alcoholics than non-secret, a consideration which, if valid, would toss into a cocked hat the 1 to 6 ratio mentioned above.

Dorothy A is a secret drinker. To her friends, should they ever learn of it, this would be most astonishing. They would be inclined to give any such report the lie, for in their experience Miss A drinks very sparingly indeed. When she is invited out for the evening, she may accept one drink, but she will sip at it and toy with it all evening. Or she may refuse even the one drink. She is successful in seeming poised and quietly reserved.

She attends to the conversation, and when she chooses to participate she always, her friends will tell you, makes a contribution. They have respect for her cool intelligence and apparently detached calm. In fact, however, as Miss A sits, not moving often, never restless, quietly attentive, she is inside a seething wrangle of tensions; and when, later, she bids her escort good-night and locks herself alone inside her apartment, as like as not she may proceed to drink herself blind drunk to appease those internal conflicts.

They are complex, her internal conflicts. Her mother, when Miss A was still a baby, used always to sit by her bedside until she was asleep. Sometimes, if she was frightened, her mother would hold her hand. (In analysis, when she experienced a frightening emotion, Miss A would involuntarily reach her hand out to the analyst, seeking the same comfort.) As she grew up, Miss A found that she had grown to depend on a protective union with others. When she first drank, her need for such union led to sexual intercourse. The experience gave her both pleasure and guilt. When it was repeated, a year or so later, again after she had been drinking, she grew frightened. But fright was precisely what had, in the first instance, led her to seek the magical protective union with her mother's hand. She was plunged deeper into her behavioral dilemma.

For a time, her solution was to abjure alcoholic beverages utterly. As a solution, it was effective up to the moment when she discovered that she was prone to seek the same protective union, and with a comparative stranger, without a drop of liquor to lower, as she thought, her guard.

Frightened, she used a sexual partner the way, as a child, she had used her mother's protective hand: to comfort her, to drive away her anxieties. Now, as then, it was a narcissistic need, and only her sturdy superego kept her from quieting her fears more and more often in the same promiscuous way. Her drinking, however, did not so much concern her superego. Her father had, after all, himself been an excessive drinker, so that the excessive use of liquor seemed a very permissible thing to Miss A. She was by now launched on a successful merchandising career, and this set up another fear: that she would surpass her father, who had been a business failure.

Denied recourse to sexual adventures by her own inner censor, but once again experiencing unconscious fears that nagged at her to restore her self-esteem, Miss A resumed her drinking. An interlude of sex had always reassured her, had always demonstrated that, yes, she was attractive, someone did "love" her; a sexual experience was for her, then, only pseudo-sexual, but in reality narcissistic. Alcohol pampered, as her sexual partners had done, her narcissistic needs. There was only one danger: she recognized that she must be careful to see to it that alcohol did not again lead her into the same misadventures that once it had. And so, with that alarm bell ringing in her unconscious, she has taken to locking herself alone in her apartment. For her, it is not a slip to drink; a slip is to drink and discover that the drink has led her out on the town and into the arms of some man, any man. She has had, since she has come into psychoanalysis, no such slips (a matter of nearly two years). And the only ones who share her knowledge that she engages in her secret drinking bouts are her close-mouthed maid and her analyst.

Will her bouts continue? It is impossible to be sure, although as these words are written there has been no need for Miss A to drink for more than three months. It is a very short time; and it may end tomorrow; but there is every likelihood that it will not. For with each passing day she gains additional insight into the complex of difficulties that occasionally has led her to put her trust in the self-betraying drug that is alcohol.

Such insights come hard. Beatrice W, for example, believed that there was only one reason why she had a problem with alcohol: it was because she had suddenly learned that the man who was her lover had been married seven years to another woman, was the father of two children, and had not the slightest desire to divorce his wife so that he might marry Miss W.

It is always difficult to credit the existence of such a liaison. Every now and then we read about such a thing in the newspapers, but surely most of us decline to believe it. How is it possible for a woman not to *know* her lover is married to another woman? She must, we feel, be purposely blinding herself to the facts. Unconsciously, we insist, she must realize that he will never be able to marry her; and that is why, masochistically, she has launched herself in his direction. The affair is star-crossed from the outset.

But Miss W's story did seem credible. When she had met him, he was in Paris, thousands of miles away from his family, and able to devote himself wholeheartedly to her. Nor was there ever a chink in the armor of his lies until the moment when, on the last day of her unscheduled week's visit to New York, Miss W got a phone call from his wife. Then she knew and then, she said later, she started drinking.

It had been, she claimed, an entirely successful and gratifying love affair. She had never, until the moment of her discovery, had any particular desire to drink. Even if she had, she said, she would not have done so, for *he* didn't like her when she drank. So even her occasional social drinks she drank only when she was apart from him. That is the substance of what she said at her first interview.

At her second interview, it developed that this unmarried, thirty-five-year-old woman had done a considerable amount of fairly hard drinking when she was in her twenties. At that time she had been under pressure from her parents to get married, who held up to her, as an ideal, the marriage of her sister —sixteen months younger, livelier, and—in her eyes—prettier and in every social way more desirable.

A psychiatrist, probing into the emotional experiences of a patient, is rather (one might think) like an archaeologist digging away at the layers of a nation's history, in a city so antique that he dare not guess what he will find. Should he stop at this level, fearful that if he digs further his proof of this level's antiquity will crumble and disappear? Comparably, should the psychiatrist be satisfied to establish that Miss W had drunk hard and addictively during her middle twenties because she had a younger sister whom she considered prettier and more charming? And should the psychiatrist focus all therapeutic measures at that level?

But the example is a poor one: the analogy does not hold. For the archaeologist can fix his layers of earth, his evidence of human existence. The psychiatrist, convinced that a patient's addictive drinking has a cause far deeper-seated than an unhappy love affair of her thirties, far deeper-seated than a sibling rivalry of her twenties or teens, may nevertheless be unable to bring the patient back to the point where *she* will see, in the layers of her earthly experience, the evidence of the origin of her neurosis. The psychiatrist may, after a dozen interviews, be wholly persuaded that a Miss W's addictive drinking stems from her pronounced dependency; but such a conviction will be worthless unless the Miss W can be brought to appreciate its validity.

In Miss W's case, this has not yet happened.

Virginia L is an extremely attractive woman in her forties, who has been married for about twenty years. She was the youngest of five children born to a wealthy family of old

American stock. For several generations this family has lived in or near Boston; they were staid, decent, able, intelligent folk, models of what the descendants of Puritan settlers should be. Virginia L can point back to jurists, governors, admirals, and bishops on her family tree; but she is a lady of liberal temperament and prefers to live in the present and plan for the future.

She married well. Her husband is a successful corporation lawyer—at least, that is what the world sees. Mrs. L sees deeper and clearer: she sees a man who is often troubled and sometimes in despair as he attempts to cope with the unconscious forces that surge within him. She looks on him with much compassion but with, as well, much irritation. Her irritation is quick to flare up and difficult for her to control.

And yet their marriage has always seemed conspicuously happy. They have lived at proper urban addresses, summered at proper resorts, consorted with proper people, and pursued, alone and in company, the proper and socially acceptable customs of their circle and their time. As far as liquor is concerned, they had it to offer their guests during Prohibition and afterwards; they drank lightly and irregularly; they saw nothing particularly amusing about drunkenness, nor did they cherish the notion of awaking with a hangover; they had the practice of serving wine with their meals when they were entertaining; no more than two martinis before dinner and perhaps a relaxed brandy or whisky highball after dinner; a couple, one would have remarked, with a civilized and moderate attitude toward alcohol.

And yet Virginia L, belatedly, found that she was an alcoholic. She made the discovery after some fifteen years of married life. How did this come about?

The discovery itself she made easily enough. There was nothing difficult about that, although the process was painful.

The time came, and in her life it was when she was forty-one, when she found she could not see her husband off to work soon enough, so that she might be alone to plan, in fantasy, how she would start to drink. At first her drinking was solitary and began around four in the afternoon; later it started at noon, or even earlier, and by choice she had someone around to drink with her. The someone might be her mother, but by preference it was someone of her own generation; and Mrs. L liked to think that whoever it was did not realize that alcohol was involved. The companion was invited over for coffee or for tea, and that was what the companion got; but in Mrs. L's cup there was, in addition, a good strong slug of whisky.

By the time her husband came home from his office, Mrs. L would be pretty well mulled. This practice became regular enough, in her life, so that, being an intelligent woman, she was forced to think about it, to wonder why, and then to try and stop it. It was when she found that she could not stop it that she realized she was an alcoholic.

No, the discovery itself was not difficult. But how had it come about that she, a happy woman, happily born into a good and well-circumstanced family, happily married to a successful man, should have tripped over this unlikely and unseemly symptom?

The words *happy* and *happily* are, of course, used with some irony, and can be accurately applied to Mrs. L's circumstances only on the superficial level. As always, the truth is hard to come by, and in the compass of these pages there is no opportunity for a detailed search. We can only suggest where the truth may be hiding and, in very oversimplified fashion, hint at the sources of Mrs. L's misery.

Her parents had the practice of keeping their newest-born in their bedroom, for so long as there was not another baby born to dislodge the incumbent. In Virginia's case, she was at length dispatched to her own room, but only after a longer stay than usual, for she was the baby of the family. Just as, in connection with weaning, Freud wrote, "No matter how long the child lived on the mother's breast, he will always carry the conviction, after the weaning, that it was too short and too little," so, despite her rather longer than usual period close to her parents, for Virginia it was over too soon.

But as the official baby of a large family, she was afforded ample opportunity to luxuriate in a state of narcissism. Nor was there anything important that occurred in her childhood to deal a severe blow to her self-regard. She was a bright child, and a pretty child; in college she was an able student and a popular date; she made a lovely bride, and she was married to a young man whose future was full of bright promise.

During the first years of her marriage, things went smoothly. Then suddenly her narcissistic self-regard was struck hard, twice in succession. The blows came with triphammer force and they coincided with the entry of this country into the war. The first shock was when she discovered that her husband had been unfaithful to her. The second came when, despite her very strong desire to have a baby, her husband dramatized his refusal to father a baby by enlisting in the Marine Corps.

Alone, dislocated by his departure, Mrs. L closed her apartment in New York and went to work in Philadelphia. Her pathological drinking dates from this period, and to this period, as well, belongs her own faithless sexual behavior. The two are linked in her mind. She believes that the moral breakdown exemplified by her entering into a wartime love affair occasioned simultaneously a moral breakdown in relation to drinking.

But both stem from the fact of her having sustained two well-nigh mortal wounds to her self-esteem.

She was forced to face two very unpleasant truths: she could not have all that she wished either as a wife or as a mother.

It is difficult to conceive of a more unpalatable dish for a woman to have to swallow. The effect on her ego was traumatic. While sympathizing with her for the pain we can be sure she suffered, we must also take note of what happened to her particular predisposing traits as a result of the pain: at a time when her self-esteem was grievously wounded, the unconscious system of her mind generated a memory-pattern; unconsciously she recalled how, in the period of her primary narcissism, whenever she had felt so wounded, magically her cry had effected the appearance of a something that soothed and warmed and restored her self-esteem.

In the same fashion she now found that alcohol would restore her self-esteem. She had never needed alcohol to perform this service for her before. Her drinking was qualitatively different now, from what it had been during the early years of her married life. She had been drunk only once in her youth: that was at a New Year's Eve party when her host insisted she drink rather more champagne than she should have, and she got first tipsy and then sick. But in Philadelphia she began getting drunk in earnest, as a method of healing the wounds to her self-esteem. It was, to be sure, a very misleading and meretricious method, and it worked for only a short time, but no matter, when the pain came to be felt again, the same method could be tried again, the same medicine was ready at hand.

Mrs. L sought help when she realized she was an alcoholic and, in a measure, she has got it. She has mastered her symptom. Once only has she tripped. It happened in this way:

She was walking along a city street, in the afternoon, when all of a sudden she experienced an overwhelming desire for a drink. Without a further thought, she turned into a hotel, took a room, was shown upstairs, and promptly picked up the phone and ordered from room service a fifth of whisky, some ice, and some soda. Then, her hands trembling, she lay down on the bed to wait. Room service was slow.

Desperately, Mrs. L thought back, striving to understand whence her sudden impulse had come. What had happened? What had she been doing? What had she been thinking? She forced herself, with an almost physical act of mental self-discipline, to try to remember.

She had been on an errand. She had been headed for the cleaner's to pick up her husband's brown tweed suit so that she could pack it for him. He was flying to Chicago next morning on business. What had she been thinking about? Nothing. She couldn't remember. But there must have been something on her mind, her mind couldn't have been a total blank. Let's see. She turned off the avenue, into the side street, went past the apartment building and then past the shop where a hairdresser had a few months ago opened a beauty parlor. His name was Rudolph. "& Rudolph" she called his establishment, to herself: this was because when it had first been opened it was a partnership, Somebody & Rudolph, but they must have had a fight for Somebody's name had been taken off the sign. The lettering on the door had never been repainted, however; centered on the glass pane, it read:

Rudolph
All Styles of Hairdressing

Forever off-balance. What was the name of that partner? She couldn't remember.

There was a knock at her door, and here came room service, with the whisky and the ice. Distractedly, Mrs. L paid him, but she did not open the bottle. What was the partner's name? It was true; now she could remember: she *had* noticed that off-center lettering. And it must have been right after that that she suddenly felt she must have a drink.

On a thought, she went to the bedside night-table, found a

classified telephone directory, turned to "Beauty Shops," and —there were nine pages of them. She looked at the whisky bottle for a moment and then turned with determination to the nine pages of names. She was still on the first column when she suddenly remembered. The name of the ex-partner was Elaine. Elaine and Rudolph. And why shouldn't she have forgotten the name Elaine, she reflected bitterly, since it was also the name of the secretary with whom, years ago, her husband had been unfaithful, during just such a business trip as the one he was now preparing to take?

Alone in the hotel room, Mrs. L understood that her ungovernable impulse to have a drink was her unconscious response to a reminder of the hurt she had received. And her husband was leaving, now, for another three days away from her. Might he not again hurt her as he had before? Some such fear had clenched its fist, deep in her unconscious, and driven her here to this hotel room.

In some triumph, Mrs. L brought the story and the unopened bottle of whisky to her analyst, to prove that she had tripped but not quite fallen.

We have said that the predisposing traits are dynamic, and we have urged that there are many alcoholics who would never have been caught up in the grip of their impulse neurosis had it not been for some set of circumstances uniquely contrived to seek out and damage the already vulnerable. Mrs. L, it would seem, neatly illustrates the point. It is of course ridiculous to assume that she had moved through thirty or thirty-five years of life without encountering people who said cruel things, things that hurt her; without being faced by situations calculated to upset her, damage her narcissistic self-esteem. But her ego was strong enough and well enough developed so that she could ignore such affronts and overcome such dangers. It required two sudden and devastating blows to crumble her defenses.

Now, in analysis, she is in the process of rebuilding her defenses and, it is to be hoped, on a sounder foundation.

III

It must be clear to the most casual observer that alcoholism affects its victims in strikingly different ways. In the gallery of quick sketches through which we have just passed, for instance: one drank hard for twenty years before discovering that his drinking was beyond his control; another drank sparingly, almost abstemiously, for a dozen or more years before suddenly plunging into addictive drinking; a third was never able to drink very hard; a fourth has never known what it was to be temperate. Some experienced blackouts, some did not; some sneaked drinks, some did not. And so on. Nor was there any effort to select, for that group, men and women whose approach to alcohol was notably various or in whom the symptom would highlight obvious distinguishing patterns of behavior. They were truly chosen at random. If it had been otherwise, there would have been included among them a drinker of the typical Skid Row type (not all of whom, by any means, live on Skid Row), and perhaps as well a psychotic, for whom drinking is symptomatic of a far more serious mental disorder than any we have encountered in this book.

Alcoholics are different, and their differences have been noted, catalogued, and fitted into several systems of classification. We earlier mentioned the confusion that has attended on the several efforts to classify types of excessive drinking. Now we submit such a system, and we claim for it two virtues.

Originality is not one of them. Indeed, to strive to be original, in an area where so many have been successful in being merely unique, is no virtue. The virtues of our system are: (1) it follows, in broad outline, the suggestions put forward by the Alcoholism Subcommittee of the Expert Committee on Mental Health of the World Health Organization, and (2) it is both reasonable and inclusive. It is high time that a measure of unified thinking begin to pervade the world of those who are attempting to help or at least cope with excessive drinkers, and it seems to us that as good a place as any to start is with the international organization which has accepted the responsibility of coordinating all the expert, specialized opinion in this field. Fortunately, in addition, the signposts erected by the WHO's Alcoholism Subcommittee are sensible.

And some sort of signposts are an absolute necessity, for without classification there can be no proper diagnosis and, thereafter, no proper therapy.

This system of classification, then, divides all excessive drinkers into three categories:

1. Irregular symptomatic excessive drinkers.
2. Habitual symptomatic excessive drinkers.
3. Addictive drinkers (alcohol addicts).

Of these, only the latter two groups are alcoholics.

Here are three categories, and we propose to complicate (and, we hope, simultaneously clarify) the picture by subdividing each of them so that we will end with six categories. But before we do so, we must call attention to some of the words used in the descriptions.

To begin with, we are concerned only with the *excessive* drinkers, the drinkers whose habits cause themselves or society a problem. The vast bulk of us who drink do so, clearly, without creating any such problems. Who can legitimately oppose A's desire to drink a Beaujolais or a California Pinot Noir with his rare sirloin of beef? Who will legitimately object to B's wish to cool his throat, during a seventh-inning stretch, with a can of beer right off the ice? Who will deny C's right to toast his bride in champagne? Or D's civilized practice of mixing even a hideously dry martini and drinking it before he tackles his meal? It is only the man, woman, or child who goes further and blinds himself, drowns his sense of personal conduct, obliterates his intelligence, and dissolves his superego with whom we are concerned. This is the *excessive* drinker.

The word *symptomatic* is not so easily clarified, especially inasmuch as we have already pointed out that *all* drinking, *all* reference to alcoholic beverages, is symptomatic—symptomatic of our accedence to social customs and, more importantly, symptomatic of the influence of our unconscious mental systems over us all. But in the sense in which the WHO's experts use the word, it means symptomatic of some inner individual tension, some conflict for which relief is sought through drinking. And so it shall here.

The connotations of the word *addictive*, especially as distinguished from *compulsive* and from *habit-forming*, must also be discussed, but we will reserve comment on this point for a moment and turn to a consideration of the three categories listed above and to the subdivisions which we believe they must include.

1. What sets the irregular symptomatic excessive drinker apart from the excessive drinkers who must be considered alcoholics is his ability to stop his drinking if necessary and in any event to control it. (Throughout this discussion the masculine pronoun will be used; this is only a convenience; the feminine pronoun, it should be understood, is interchangeable with the masculine.)

He may be what is usually called a *heavy social drinker*. If so, he is probably, although not necessarily, a daily drinker, the kind of person who may drink one or more cocktails before lunch, two or three or more cocktails before dinner, and perhaps as well several highballs after dinner. Often by bedtime he is drunk, but he holds his liquor well and knows how to be careful when he begins to feel the effects of his load. He experiences hangovers but rarely resorts to a hair of the dog that bit him. He manages to take care of his work in spite of not feeling up to par, and neither he nor his employer attributes his occasional inefficiency to alcohol—at least not for many years.

While he might not go so far as to feel that no occasion can be fun without alcohol, certainly he prefers those occasions when it is served, and he is quite likely to drink as though afraid he may not get his share. (This is especially true of him when the liquor belongs to someone else.) He sees no harm in it, feels no apparent guilt about it, and, while he says he can take it or leave it, usually takes it.

He may become a dull companion, as the years roll on, for heavy doses of alcohol are not compatible with intellectual or esthetic interests; but he does not, typically, react to their loss with dismay. He may spend too much of his income on liquor, which may in turn cause himself and his family minor deprivations; he may fail to advance in his business or profession; but by and large he is likely to get by for many years without much change in his drinking pattern. In his late forties or fifties, however, he is likely to develop physical ailments, perhaps one of the neuropathies, or a fatty or cirrhotic liver, for even the hardiest constitution cannot stand up forever under the incessant assaults of a toxic compound.

But when he is told by his doctor that he must curtail or even halt his drinking altogether, he is able to do it. He will hate it, but he will be able to do it. Logic gets through to him. He is not the slave of his unconscious. An important part of his motivation to drink is conscious. He may be neurotic; he may have unconscious goals; but alcohol is not for him the necessary means by which he strives to attain them.

He may also be the sort of drinker who drinks hard but only occasionally. The word occasionally is here used in two senses: it refers both to celebratory occasions and to those irregular times when—either because of the pressure of mounting tensions or because of some one particularly excessive stress—he seems to set out almost deliberately to get drunk, to anesthetize himself. So, it may be a convention, a wedding, an alumni reunion, an anniversary, or even an apparently ordinary Saturday night party which has taken on some special significance for him. At such a time he constitutes at best a nuisance and at worst a menace—both on the highways and in the living room. Or, on the other hand, it may be the heartbreak occasioned by the loss of a wife (or a husband) or a child or a parent; or the loss of a job on which all his hopes were pinned; or some other sort of blow to his security, emotional or financial. The occasion may be anniversarial or it may be the result of some deep inner conflict. Sometimes, by some writers, if it is the latter case, he is referred to as a situational drinker, and he is discussed as though his problems were addictive but in some unknown and wonderful way disappeared so that he was able to resume social drinking.

There may be such a person as the *situational drinker*. Indeed, we are tempted to say that there must be such a type, for its existence is postulated by so many who have studied the varieties of problem drinking carefully. At the same time, out of a series of eight hundred and fifty excessive drinkers, carefully studied for drinking pattern as well as for sociological and psychological background, not one was found who could be so classified. It is at best a dubious classification. Earlier we mentioned how, in the case of some individuals, it is possible that a special set of circumstances may arise in the life situation so as to overwhelm the previously vulnerable personality. It seems likely that the situational drinker, he who has lost control over his drinking temporarily because of personal tragedy, deep humiliation, severe financial reverse, or other seriously upsetting event, is a person who is precisely *not* previously vulnerable, but has within him the predisposing traits to a lesser degree. In him, and only very temporarily, the upsetting event has the effect of enhancing those traits: he becomes their momentary victim, but not for long; his ego strength is such that he can, when the shock of the event is absorbed, return to his former habits, including his former drinking habits.

But—and especially because, as we have said, the predisposing traits are always dynamic—we must again insist that any heavy drinker, of whatever type, is potentially an addictive drinker.

It depends. Some very respected clinicians in the field of alcoholism insist categorically that if an individual drinks hard enough and long enough he will become addicted to the use of alcohol. Insofar as this conditional statement casts doubt on the strength of the individual's ego structure, there can be no question about its validity. In any event, the irregular symptomatic excessive drinker is vulnerable. Whether he drinks heavily every day or drinks excessively only occasionally, there is always the possibility that the pharmocological property of the drug may so operate as to transfer him from the first category to the second or to the third.

How many of those who drink are to be included in this first category? That is to say, how many drinkers, by drinking excessively, may endanger their own health and the well-being or even the lives of some of the rest of us? There is no way of answering this question accurately. We know that these excessive drinkers are responsible for most of the arrests for drunkenness, for an appreciable amount of the traffic fatalities, for a considerable part of the total of industrial accidents—in short, for a lot of social misery. Just how much it is impossible to say.

2. The category of habitual symptomatic excessive drinkers must be subdivided into two separate and entirely different groupings.

The first is numerically less significant and is certainly less well known to the average citizen. It includes the *psychotic drinkers*—to put it more accurately, the people suffering from one of the well-recognized grave mental illnesses, usually either paranoid schizophrenia or manic-depressive reaction, whose use of alcohol is regular, excessive, and a symptom of their disorder.

It should be emphasized that the use of alcohol is, for these seriously sick, not the cause of their psychosis but only its symptom. Addictive alcoholics are liable to psychotic episodes and to psychosis if the cycle of their addiction cannot in some way be broken. But this end result should not be confused with the psychosis in which excessive drinking is a symptom.

The psychodynamics that lead to the choice of excessive drinking as a symptom by those suffering from these severe maladies have as yet not been sufficiently explored. But it is pertinent to point out that in the case both of schizophrenia and of the manic-depressive reaction a cardinal factor is regressive narcissism.

Often, with the schizophrenic, his symptoms are apparent only during intoxication and disappear with the return of sobriety, with the result that they are excused on the grounds of chronic alcoholism or, worse, on the grounds simply of drunkenness. This sort of faulty diagnosis—or, as is more often the case, this total absence of diagnosis—is responsible for some of the more chaotic and violent crimes that occasionally erupt on the front pages of our daily newspapers.

The schizophrenic is more likely to give way to vicious emotional outbursts, to bizarre behavior, to perverse and promiscuous sexual behavior, and to suicidal attempts and actual suicide, than is the addictive drinker.

For the manic-depressive, alcohol is an extremely useful tool to shorten and alleviate, while complicating, the deep depression which is usually typical. And the manic phase is marked by more excitement, more bizarre behavior than is customary for the addictive drinker.

Nor, indeed, is the use of alcohol by these seriously sick people addictive. As soon as their malady has been properly diagnosed, as soon as therapy is instituted, their dependence on alcohol disappears. To be sure, such therapy is usually institutional, which in turn means that there is very little opportunity for them to have access to alcohol. But even taking this into consideration, their relationship to the drug is not marked by the overwhelming impulses that are the hallmark of the addictive drinker.

In the second grouping of habitual symptomatic excessive drinkers are the *Skid Row drinkers*, the social misfits familiar to every urban inhabitant or visitor. These are the unfortunates—we are inclined to think of them in stereotyped fashion as bums, panhandlers, winos, the dregs of society, and all of these conceptions are erroneous—who for many years were summoned up by the mind's eye whenever the word "alcoholic" was used. Actually, while their drinking is pathological, it is markedly different from addictive drinking, so much so that it warrants some special examination.

One prefatory word of caution: There has been far too little diagnostic research into the causal aspects of Skid Row drinking. This is, when you think of it, quite natural. The men who inhabit Skid Row are so withdrawn from society, so difficult of access by a therapist, so brutalized and ignored by society, and so incapable of seeking assistance that they have been the last for whom medicine has been able to formulate any diagnostic or therapeutic approach. This is the sad truth, despite the fact that the Skid Row drinkers stick out like sore thumbs, or rather like open, festering sores, right under society's very nose, and have for generations. The Salvation Army, and especially its dedicated social service workers, have done yeoman work among the Skid Row drinkers; and latterly the sociologists have interested themselves in these outcasts of society. But there is still far too little known about their lives, their drinking habits, and, most important of all, the psychic damage that underlies both.

In order to understand the pathology of the Skid Row drinker's relationship to alcohol, we must first differentiate between two concepts which seem at first blush to be simply two different ways of describing the same thing. One is loss of control, the other is inability to stop. These phrases represent the best effort of experts to describe two quite different patterns of pathological drinking, even marked by quite different syndromes.

By loss of control is meant the pattern of behavior, restricted to the addictive drinker, in which once drinking has been started it will not stop until the individual is so drunk or so sick that he can no longer swallow another drink. The onset of loss of control marks, in the history of the addictive drinker, the beginning of the crucial phase of his neurosis, when the symptom first gathers him into its grip. It marks as well, to borrow the concept first elucidated by Sándor Radó, the end of the realistic regime of the ego and the beginning of the pharmacothymic regime of the ego. This loss of control may result in a bout of drinking that will last a few hours or a few days; its duration is not so important as the fact that, once begun, the drinker is helpless to stop it until he is physically unable to protract it any further.

Such a bout may be succeeded by weeks or even months of abstention, depending on the impact of the drinker's remorse, the state of his pocketbook, and, most importantly, the state of his internal tensions. But when, for no matter what reason, whether it be because of a social situation or an inner conflict, he takes his next drink, once again his loss of control dictates that he will drink and drink on until once again he is physically unable to swallow another drop.

With inability to stop, on the other hand, the drinker never loses control. Always he regulates his alcoholic intake. He may have reached the stage at which he drinks steadily—from the time he gets up in the morning until the time he goes to bed at night, day after day, every day of his life—but he can control how much he drinks.

Among drinkers who have lost control, blackouts are frequent. Among those unable to stop, the blackout is a rarity. Those who have lost control are of course keenly aware of their behavior pattern; in fighting against it they may be able to abstain from alcohol for fairly long periods before the situation arises in which they justify by rationalization the one or two drinks that precipitate another bout. Those who are unable to stop, on the other hand, often feel no particular need to change their drinking habits. Their periods of abstinence almost never come about as a result of any inner effort to combat their dependence on alcohol, but rather because of social pressure brought on them from without.

Someone hit upon a vivid way to differentiate between the two types of habitual excessive drinking behavior: those who have lost control are called *peak drinkers*, those who are unable to stop *plateau drinkers*.

The distinction is no quibble. Both are considered alcoholics, but only the peak drinkers, those who lose control, are believed to be truly addictive.

With this distinction in mind, let us return to Skid Row for a look at its inhabitants and, as a first step, let us reject the phrase "Skid Row drinker" as both insufferably disparaging and inaccurate to boot. A better term would be "homeless men."

Because they are homeless, apparently aimless and rootless, and in any event cut off from normal social bonds, the tendency is to think of them as deviant individuals who, rejecting or rejected by society, can not or choose not to form any alliances whatever. The sociologists who have made a study of the homeless men have taught us differently.

When a man lands on Skid Row, he does make attachments. He gravitates to other, like-minded men. Groups are formed, on an informal and casual basis to be sure, numbering anywhere from four to eight or ten. In addition there are a very few lone wolves, but the typical homeless man has his regular circle of friends and associates. There are, in this social pale, even recognizable strata, based on the preferences and snobbisms of experience or habit or mode of life. The common denominator for all is the inability to adjust to the demands of a complex society, and the consequent withdrawal to a world in which few demands are made, no responsibilities attach, no consistent effort is required, ambition is forgotten, and society may be ignored.

Most of these men were emotionally dislocated early in life. When they were still children their homes were broken up for any of a variety of reasons. Most of them have known institutional life in some form: jail, prison, reformatory, city shelter, orphan's home, hospital. Many of them have known no other life.

Most of them drink. There are a few who do not, but even of these the majority have had a drinking problem at some time in their lives. Moreover, an appreciable number of them drink with loss of control (which is one of the reasons why the term "Skid Row drinker" is inaccurate as applied to the drinker who, while never experiencing loss of control, is nevertheless unable to stop). But it seems to be the case that the greater number of these homeless men are not addictive. Their pathological drinking is marked only by inability to stop.

Typically, a group of half a dozen men drinks in this way: One or two of their number are informally delegated, on a rotating basis, to get some money (either by panhandling, or by taking an odd job, or by selling their blood by the pint); this money is used to buy a quart or a half-gallon of fortified wine; and the bottle is thereafter shared among the members of the group until it is gone. Drinking so, the plateau drinker can guard his supply for many hours: he takes his nips steadily but spaces them. Where the plateau drinker and his companions will be able to swig from the same half-gallon bottle for a day or more, the alcohol addict will empty the fifth of whisky in a couple of hours.

Clearly, the type of drink plays an important part in differentiating these drinking patterns. And the difference extends beyond our own American cultural boundaries. In this country the excessive drinker's preference is for distilled spirits, and more excessive drinkers exhibit loss of control than inability to stop. But overseas, and especially in the wine-growing countries, the reverse is the case. In France, for example, it is reported that the majority of habitual excessive drinkers, who quite naturally drink wine by choice, are plateau drinkers; and amnesic episodes, blackouts, are comparatively rare except in the late stages of alcoholism.

It is as though the tensions, the internal conflicts that threaten to overwhelm the plateau drinker can by him be abated if only he can maintain the level of alcohol in his bloodstream at a relatively steady and relatively low ratio.

Some there are, by no means homeless men, who are given to this drinking pattern. We are thinking of Charlotte B who, every day of her life, drinks regularly from the time she gets up to the time when at length she is able to fall asleep. Moreover, she drinks spirits. Her morning coffee is laced with rum or whisky, not for medicinal hair-of-the-dog reasons, but simply to abate her psychic jitters. During the course of her average day, she will drink between ten and thirty ounces of spirits, usually slowly, usually slightly diluted. On occasion she may increase her consumption, but even then she never loses control. She is always just a trifle mulled: never sober, never falling-down drunk; always able to talk, always able to discharge her household duties on a minimal basis, and always intent on sedating herself. Whether, as the years go on, her pattern will stay the same cannot be predicted. She has drunk so for twelve years, and in that time has experienced blackouts only three or four times. Her drinking is not surreptitious nor particularly avid, but it is necessary to her and she is sufficiently aware of its pathological aspects so that she has regularly recurring feelings of guilt about it, although not to the point of putting up any fight against it. It is part of her life. Without its assistance she cannot or thinks she cannot face the world, the flesh, and the devil that torments her internally. Since it is also a pleasurable necessity, a soothing potion, and in consequence difficult for her to forswear, it is doubtful that any sort of psychotherapy would by now be of service in helping her exorcise her inner demon. Her will to get well has been sapped. Her best hope lies in institutional treatment if she is ever to be wholly rehabilitated.

Under the steady, drumming attacks of alcohol on her ego

structure, there is no question but what Charlotte B would deteriorate just as have most of the homeless men, were it not for her relatively secure social position. Physically and mentally she is damaging herself, but socially she is protected; and so long as she is able to keep from losing control she will continue to be able to function, however submarginally.

3. And so we come to the alcohol addict, the addictive drinker, the one whose drinking habits and patterns have become, especially in the last decade, the subject of so much attention, in novels like *The Lost Weekend*, plays like *The Country Girl*, in movies, radio, and television programs, and in the daily press. Here too it is not only convenient but, we feel, more accurate to set up two groupings—the primary addicts and the secondary addicts.

From the point of view of their drinking patterns, the two are distinctly different. The *primary addict*, from his first introduction to beverage alcohol, uses it as an aid to adjust to his environment. From the outset it is for him a magical substance. Only through the use of intoxicants can he achieve a state of psychological harmony—a very deceptive harmony it is, and a very transitory one. He craves the effect that alcohol produces, and is able to obtain it with a relatively small dosage. His addiction is, if unchecked, rapid; his submission to a pharmacothymic regime likewise rapid; his need for therapy is evidenced within a matter of a very few years, perhaps within months.

The *secondary addicts* do not, from the outset, show the same psychological dependence on the drug. They pursue, often for many years, a program of heavy social drinking. While they are still young they have—or rather, swiftly develop—a considerable tolerance for alcohol and often drink prodigious amounts. Superficially they are, in contradistinction to the primary addicts, well adjusted to their environment;

many have excelled in their work and many have very real accomplishments behind them. Their addiction may not begin until after twenty or even more years of fairly steady, fairly hard drinking.

The reason for the difference resides in the psychodynamic feature which we have already had occasion to describe: the fact that the predisposing traits are never static, but always either in growth or in decline.

The primary addict is one in whom the predisposing traits are so developed and so sharply marked that his first recourse to this socially approved narcotic is only a matter of time. He may have a very low sense of self-esteem, while always in his unconscious there lurks the memory of the time when he was omnipotent. So, he may experience apprehension about his first job: can he compete successfully? Dare he? Whom is he fooling? Can't everyone around him, his boss, his foreman, his co-workers, can't they all see that he is scared, nervous, inefficient, putting up a bluff, lacking in talent? If he has no relish for the competitive way of American business life, he will have recourse to liquor just so soon as he receives the impulse from his unconscious, from the echo-chamber of his inadequately experienced emotions, that reminds him of his unconscious and symbolic goal: invulnerability, omnipotence.

Or perhaps his apprehension stems from a fear of inadequacy in his social and sexual relationships. He has a need to instill confidence in himself, before he can face a date; but instead of instilled confidence, here, so easy to his hand, is distilled confidence. Now he can be as charming as the hero of a Hollywood movie; now he can be witty; now he need not care that he never learned how to dance properly or say the right things, or was able to wear the right clothes.

In the case of the primary addict, the decisive symptom, loss of control, appears early in his drinking history. Thereafter his own sense of self-esteem, depreciated to begin with, will take a merciless pounding not only from himself but from those around him—his dismayed family, his impatient employer, and so on. If he thought he was unworthy before, now he is given proof. He is threatened and punished in a myriad ways. His security, both financial and emotional, is either weakened or disappears altogether. It is for him an intolerable state of affairs and so he attempts to drown his misery anew.

The secondary addict, on the other hand, has achieved an appreciably greater degree of emotional maturity. His infantile traits in abeyance, he is able to pursue his course in life apparently unhindered by his use of alcohol. His success or failure is not related to his drinking, except perhaps very indirectly. During this time, he drinks about as the social customs of his group dictate, maybe a little more. But inside him, something is happening.

He has within him strong impulses demanding discharge. Some of them he is able to repress and restrain, often for a long period of time. The psychoanalyst would refer to undischarged instinctual excitation. Many psychiatrists have remarked, using different terminology, a mental phenomenon by means of which we are able to get rid of tensions built up by some external stimulation and, having banished them, return to an energy state of equilibrium. Freud referred to this equilibrium as the Nirvana principle; others have adopted a term from physiology and call it homeostasis. In the physiological sense, homeostasis describes the internal systems of stabilization which man has evolved in order to survive—constancy of temperature, of water, of sugar, of oxygen, of calcium, and so on. The French physiologist Claude Bernard summed up homeostasis in a celebrated aphorism: "La fixité du milieu intérieur est la condition de la vie libre," and the American physiologist Walter B. Cannon wrote, commenting on this freedom: "Organisms, composed of material which is characterized by the utmost inconstancy and unsteadiness, have somehow learned the methods of maintaining constancy and keeping steady in the presence of conditions which might reasonably be expected to prove profoundly disturbing."

Our daily life is filled with incidents which at least hold the possibility of being profoundly disturbing to our mental and emotional economy. Thanks to homeostasis, a tension or a tendency to tension is constantly being met and balanced by a contrary inhibitory tendency. A strong impulse to react to a stimulus is met by a counterforce which, if the principle of homeostasis successfully governs, will be as strong as the impulse.

A pedestrian, crossing the street at the proper crosswalk in accordance with a green light, is startled out of his wits by a horn blown by a motorist making an impatient left-hand turn. The pedestrian's impulse to the stimulus of the startling horn may be fear, which may as swiftly be transmuted into anger. Now his impulse to react will be to snarl a biting comment at the driver going past him. He may even have the impulse to run to the car, wrench open the door by the driver's side, yank the driver out into the street, and pummel the tar out of him.

Whether in fact he snarls, however, will be governed by the intensity of his original impulse and the consequent intensity of the inhibitory counterforce. As he opens his mouth to yell the well-turned and satisfactory curse, he may be arrested by the reflection that to do so is childish or, since the driver may in any case not be able to hear him, useless. He may even fleetingly consider what might happen should the driver brake his car by the curb, jump out, and run back, fists doubled, yelling in turn, "What was that you said, Jack?"

Such a homely example deals with an everyday aspect of homeostasis, but perhaps imperfectly suggests the mental economic problem involved in the individual's undischarged instinctual excitation. For the one is an isolated event, in time and in the individual's experience. But undischarged instinctual excitation properly refers to a long series of impulses, continuously demanding discharge, perhaps as continuously restrained but always with increasing difficulty. This is a process, not an isolated event.

And while this process is going on, the individual is drinking. That is to say, his undischarged excitation is interconnected with his habit of heavy social drinking.

Under the best of circumstances, it is an open question how long any individual can restrain such undischarged energy. Psychiatrists are familiar, for example, with the fact that physical change may suffice to overwhelm the counterforces inhibiting undischarged instinctual excitation. Thus, the onset of puberty, or the menopause, may for some people be enough to tip the balance of homeostasis.

The physical changes wrought by protracted heavy drinking, it is possible, are comparable. Certainly it would seem to be the case with the secondary addict. It seems a likely explanation for the large number of habitually excessive drinkers who become, with time, secondary addicts.

Some of the physical changes we have mentioned earlier, in connection with the heavy social drinker. The secondary addict will experience these, and maybe others, more serious, as well, if the cycle of his addiction is not broken in time: Korsakoff's psychosis, delirium tremens, acute hallucinosis, polyneuropathy, advanced liver disease, gross vitamin deficiency, nutritional edema, pellagra—all these lie ahead waiting for the addict who has been permitted to continue drinking into the chronic phase.

Such addiction, whether primary or secondary, is, as we have postulated earlier, neurotic in origin. There has been a considerable to-do, in many books written about alcoholism, as to whether alcoholism is a symptom or a disease entity. The matter is best resolved in this way:

Excessive drinking, whether habitual or not, is a danger signal, a symptom that all may not be well with a person's mental and psychic health. It does not follow in every case, but it may indicate that the person is neurotic, suffering from a specific disease entity, a psychoneurosis. The best qualified doctor to determine whether such excessive drinking is neurotic, which is to say, whether such drinking may become addictive, is a psychoanalyst. If the person's drinking is already addictive, it is still symptomatic, but the symptom is so gross that it must be treated all by itself, and stopped, before its roots can be explored and in turn treated.

In the past decade, the neurotic symptom has been studied with the utmost care. It has been dissected, analyzed, and broken down into its various behavioral aspects. It had to be so. It is profoundly distressing to a thoughtful person to find that someone whom he loves and respects is, all of a sudden, helpless. To turn for a moment away from the intimacy of a family circle, his readers must have been bewildered and saddened by the behavior of Scott Fitzgerald; they must have been stunned by the early and tragic death of Dylan Thomas; his audience must have been embarrassed and puzzled by the antics of John Barrymore, and must have wagged their heads when he died. These are spectacular examples, and they can be easily multiplied, too easily.

In consequence, the circumstances of the neurotic symptom have been studied. Perhaps their most careful student has been Dr. Jellinek. He has divided the drinking of the alcohol addict —whether primary or secondary—into four phases, the pre-alcoholic, the prodromal, the crucial, and the chronic. Of these, the first two he describes as purely symptomatic and the latter two as addictive. And during each phase he perceives some characteristic behavioral symptoms. Since his study is based on an analysis of the drinking histories of more than two thousand alcohol addicts, his conclusions have more than passing interest.

In the *pre-alcoholic phase*, the drinker finds rather more relief from his tensions in alcohol than does the ordinary social drinker or, as it may be, he has been able to find no other method of handling those tensions. As he finds what alcohol will do for him, so thereafter he contrives to find himself in social situations in which alcohol will be routinely offered. His tolerance to the drug increases.

The first unmistakable sign that he has entered the *prodromal phase* is the recurrent blackout. Everyone who has ever taken more drinks than he should has probably experienced the blackout, the blank, the period in which he did or said something of which he had to be reminded the next day. Of itself it can mean no more than that he had too much to drink. But if it recurs with any regularity, it is meaningful. It is accompanied, typically, by the sneaking and gulping of drinks, by preparation for a social occasion by having one or two before arriving, and by the first pangs of guilt or self-doubt in relation to alcohol. The blackout, indeed, may well be a method of dramatizing the drinker's sense of guilt—he is refusing to face his behavior, its cause, and its effect.

Loss of control is determinant. With loss of control, the drinker has entered on the *crucial stage*. Now he begins to rationalize, now his family or friends begin to warn and accuse. And, as a direct result, the drinker may now first summon up the notion of his invulnerability. He may also begin to show hostility toward any who would gainsay him, and when next morning he remembers his aggressive behavior it will entail his first real remorse.

Remorse is a further internal tension that must be satisfied somehow. How to satisfy it? He tries going on the wagon entirely, or at least tries to conduct his drinking according to various intricately prescribed rules: No morning drink, or only before dinner, or never after dinner, or only when I leave the office, or only with my wife, or no more martinis, or whatever.

Has his hostility come to a stop? Clearly not. Clearly it can, in the face of these self-deprivations, only mount. And so now he begins to be angry with the friends who counsel him, or leaves the jobs in which he has worked for critical employers. At this stage, his surging hostility often drives him to the point of physical violence. He may beat up his wife, pick quarrels with his friends that end in fist-fights, or be brought home bloody and bruised from the neighborhood saloon. In any event his drinking continues and, as it does, he loses interest in whatever had previously occupied him—whether his love for his wife, or his job, or a hobby, or the children—whatever. He begins to pity himself. He may even seek to escape his problems by moving away from them, physically moving away.

His family is, meanwhile, reacting. What can they do? Their threats, their punishments, their blandishments, their inducements to a new way of life have alike proved unavailing. They can no longer believe his promises of good behavior. Will they elect now to leave him? Or will they choose to withdraw, as he has done, within themselves, seeking to avoid future humiliation? In either case, he will resent their choice.

And, fearing their reprisals, he may begin to hide his liquor. Of course he has not been eating properly. It is at about this point that, typically, he is first hospitalized or jailed.

Whether or not this has been the case, he finds that his reliance on alcohol has led to a decrease of his sexual desire. As his sexual drive declines, his hostility toward his wife increases. Such a situation may well lead to extramarital sexuality on her part which, whether realized or fantasized, is enough to provoke his jealousy and further hostility. Indeed, he may become jealous of even the most faithful wife.

Now he may start his regular morning drinking. Now he may find himself caught up in prolonged alcoholic bouts. Now he is inviting the onset of the serious physical and mental involvements referred to earlier, which may be grouped under the heading of the alcoholic psychoses. Now he has entered the *chronic phase*. If his drinking has impoverished him and his family, it will be now that he begins to consort with drinking companions wherever he can find them—strangers in saloons, homeless men on Skid Row—and drinking alcohol in whatever form he can find it—Sterno, cough medicine, hair tonic.

Now, too, he begins to find that his hands shake, that he cannot control himself to perform the simplest sort of operation: his soup spoon may be empty by the time it reaches his mouth. He is scared, scared stiff, and ready to try anything to help himself. What has happened to his invulnerability? It is gone, gone with his tolerance to alcohol, his ability to handle the drug. He has hit bottom.

And now alcohol has completed its betrayal of him. For he has been brought to this miserable pass, curiously, through his attempts to serve the pleasure principle. He sought two opposites: he wanted to banish the painful tension of the moment and he wanted to summon euphoria. Alcohol could, it seemed to him, do both—a miracle! but alas, how short-lived.

Until fairly recently there was a notion abroad, especially cherished by a few of the older members of Alcoholics Anonymous, that a drinker had to hit bottom before he would be willing to stop drinking. This notion, like some other entrenched ideas in this complex field, is dying, but it is dying hard. More and more often, excessive drinkers who have never hit bottom and never will are turning up at alcoholism clinics or in the offices of specialists in the disorder. They are turning up before they have passed very far into the crucial phase.

Some, indeed, are applying for help while they are still in the prodromal phase. One woman came to a specialist for treatment because she had found that her drinking had begun to interfere with her enjoyment of opera. The music was important to her: she felt if she was in danger of losing that she was in danger of losing the best in her life. In comparison with what has happened to many alcoholics, her plight does not seem serious, perhaps merely trivial. Her case is, however, an example of a new phenomenon. Today, A.A. members speak of "low bottom" and "high bottom": more and more often today the drinker needs only to hit high bottom before recognizing that he needs help. It is the most encouraging consequence of the increase in public awareness of the problems posed by alcohol.

And this growing public awareness, which has taken place only in the last few years, permits us to dare predict even greater advances in public responsibility and individual concern for what has become a major American health problem.

IV

We have used the terms *drug* and *addiction* to describe alcohol and the relationship of some sick people to alcohol.

To the average person, phrases like *drug addict* or *drug addiction* usually connote such narcotics as morphine and cocaine, or heroin and opium, or marijuana. They are associated with organized crime and the underworld; they summon up a picture of such social problems as juvenile delinquency and prostitution; they are interchangeable with such sensational terms as *dope fiend*. In short, these terms have extremely ugly overtones, and their use demands brief discussion of some further questions: How comparable is alcohol addiction to narcotic addiction? Is the alcoholic in any way to be compared with the narcotic addict? What are the differences and what the likenesses?

Since any discussion of these questions is liable to explode in an emotional outburst, we must feel our way carefully. As a first step, we should settle on a sensible set of criteria which, if complied with, will describe drug addiction. Thereafter we can apply the use of alcohol and the effects of excessive use to each of the criteria, and see whether in our best judgment alcohol fits or does not fit.

Even the formulation of the criteria must, it will be recognized, be subjective. For addiction is something capricious: it involves human behavior, affecting some but not all; and the reasons why it afflicts some and not others are, to put it very mildly, not a matter of unanimous opinion. To establish a test by which alcohol shall be judged is to make a value judgment: who shall say that all subjectivity, all personal opinion and preference and emotion, has been drained out of that judgment? It is surely a difficult thing to do. In view of the social ambivalence which, as we have pointed out, is at the root of all our thinking about beverage alcohol, it may well be impossible. It is nevertheless worth the try.

Because international traffic in drugs liable to produce addiction is ominous indeed for a vulnerable society, it has for many years been a prime concern of appropriate international commissions. The World Health Organization of the United Nations has an Expert Committee concerned with problems of all sorts posed by addiction. This committee speaks with considerable authority, having in back of it the experience of generations of work done in the field by its various predecessors.

Moreover, its international character lends breadth to its formulations, and it must be remembered that the practice of taking drugs varies from one country to another: here a drug is licit, there illicit; here smoked, there eaten; here encouraged, there secret, and so on. This committee has established a definition of drug addiction, and it is worth quoting in full:

"Drug addiction is a state of periodic or chronic intoxication, detrimental to the individual and to society, produced by the repeated consumption of a drug (natural or synthetic). Its characteristics include:

(1) an overpowering desire or need (compulsion) to continue taking the drug and to obtain it by any means;

(2) a tendency to increase the dose;

(3) a psychic (psychological) and sometimes a physical dependence on the effects of the drug.

"An *addiction-producing drug* is one which produces addiction as defined. . . . Any substance which will sustain an established addiction, i.e. will adequately replace the drug which has produced the addiction, must be considered as also capable of producing an addiction."

The Expert Committee also turned its attention to drugs which might be considered habit-forming:

"A *habit-forming drug* is one which is or may be taken repeatedly without the production of all of the characteristics outlined in the definition of addiction, and which is not generally considered to be detrimental to the individual and to society."

In March, 1954, another Expert Committee, concerned with the physiological, pharmacological, and biochemical properties of alcohol, undertook to fix the position of alcohol as a drug. They worked within the framework of the definition quoted. It was their opinion that an "overpowering desire to continue taking the drug and to obtain it by any means" was a phenomenon to be noted only in a minority of the users of alcohol. Further, they argued that there is greater acquired increase of tolerance in morphinism than in alcoholism. Finally, they were persuaded that the withdrawal of alcohol from an alcohol addict resulted in nothing like the sort of symptoms that afflict the addict of the morphine drugs.

Their reasoning led them to reject the classification of alcohol as an addiction-producing drug. But they were not prepared to tuck it away among the milder, simply habit-forming drugs (like caffeine or nicotine), for they were faced with the blunt fact that alcohol, drunk excessively, too often is "detrimental to the individual and to society."

Since, in their opinion, it was neither one nor the other but an intermediate what-is-it, they agreed on this statement:

"Alcohol must be considered a drug whose pharmacological action is intermediate in kind and degree between addiction-producing and habit-forming drugs, so that compulsive craving and dependence can develop in those individuals whose make-up leads them to seek and find an escape in alcohol. With this substance the personal make-up is the determining factor but the pharmacological action plays a significant role. Damage to the individual may develop, but does so only in a minority of users. The social damage that arises extends, however, beyond these individuals themselves."

Pausing only to point out what a splendid example of the ambivalence toward alcohol we have here (at once we must have it but are fearful of it; drink it but deny it; love it and hate it; try to kill it but keep it immortal), we must turn to a closer inspection of the Expert Committee's objections.

They begin by noting that only a minority of the users of alcohol experience any overwhelming desire to continue taking the drug and to obtain it by any means. Users of morphine and its derivatives, on the other hand, are believed to experience such a desire more often than not. But is this a realistic comparison? On every hand, in our society today, we are cajoled, beseeched, implored, importuned, and begged to drink alcoholic beverages in some form or other. To avoid the blandishments one must be deaf, dumb, blind, and a hermit. It is not too much to say that things have come to the pass in some circles where the man or woman who rejects a drink is regarded askance: he is not conforming—is he queer? maybe an alcoholic? In any event, something must be wrong with him.

Let us suppose. Let us suppose that there are many companies, each goaded by the spur of competition, each dedicated to the manufacture and merchandising of the various morphine derivatives, cunningly and pleasurably disguised in candies, beverages, and cigarettes. Suppose that such were the case; suppose that social custom and tradition were in thrall to this commercial enterprise; suppose that every lure known to the gentry of the advertising business were cast in front of us to buy these candies, drinks, and smokes; suppose that these inducements were constantly before us, wherever we turned, whether in newspapers or magazines or on the radio or television or in the movies or at the houses of our dearest friends; suppose that, so far from being illegal, their use was encouraged at every turn by all the wiles of a modern nine-billion-dollar industrial giant; suppose, finally, that our government had been permissively involved in their manufacture and merchandising by virtue of an annual income of three billion dollars in taxes.

We are now in a wild world of supposition but it is nonetheless not too difficult to imagine what would happen.

A considerable number of us would feel it was wrong to take the morphinized products under any circumstances, and might even seek out quotes from Scripture to back them up. Another considerable number of us would decline, saying: "It makes me sick," or "I can't stand the taste of it." It is even barely conceivable—though hardly worth the experiment—that another and still more considerable number of us could learn to educate our tastes in such a way that we would be able to join our sociable fellows in a once-daily, or twice-weekly, or twice-monthly drink. And a rather inconsiderable number of us (although certainly more than is presently the case) * would become addicted to the substance.

If, at the same time, our society regarded alcoholic beverages with horror and forbade their usage, decrying them with even more vehemence and popular support than was the case during the years of national Prohibition, there would still be an appreciable number of us who would seek out the contraband and become addicted to its use. Because it would be inconceivably more difficult to obtain than is the case in our society today, we would say, of these addictive tipplers, that they were dope fiends, and responsible in large measure for juvenile delinquency and prostitution; and a large and thriving underworld would spring up to meet their demands.

The four paragraphs above are fantastic. But nevertheless there is in them at least an arguable truth. It is believed that the majority of us could not use opiates without becoming addicted, but this is not known. Indeed, the contrary would seem to be the case, if any of the carefully conducted and controlled experiments in this direction have any validity. Such experiments have been conducted in the medical schools of Harvard and the University of Pennsylvania among volunteer medical

* Federal Narcotics Commissioner Harry J. Anslinger, in June, 1955, estimated the number of American narcotics addicts at 60,000, or a trifle more than one for every 3,000 Americans. They are concentrated, most of them, in the urban areas around New York City, Chicago, and Los Angeles. The commissioner indicated before a Senate investigating committee that the goal was to reduce addiction to the "irreducible minimum," the level achieved between 1938 and 1948, when only one of every 10,000 Americans was an addict.

students. Healthy, normal young men who have been given opiates, so far from finding them euphoric, complain that they are nauseous, cannot understand how anyone could ever become addicted to them, and show no inclination whatsoever to try them again. If such experiments tell us anything, it is that the neurotic individual will seek out and find his symptomatic intoxicant no matter how difficult we make it for him to do so. And they tell us further that the normal, healthy individual will shun addiction, quite simply because such addiction is repellent to his ego and his superego. He cannot be tempted. Experiments in that direction are less than meaningless, they are alien to him.

Certainly the "overpowering desire to continue taking the drug and to obtain it by any means" occurs only in a minority of the users of alcohol, and certainly it is of a lesser degree than is the case with morphine. And just as certainly it is easier for the alcohol addict to obtain alcohol than it is for the morphine addict to obtain his opiate.

With the finding of the committee that acquired tolerance to alcohol is demonstrably slighter than to drugs of the morphine type there will be no argument. The morphine addict can, after long addiction, develop a tolerance to his drug that enables him to take several times the lethal dose. Despite the tales of hard drinking that abound, it is doubtful that any alcoholic could ever do the same with *his* drug.

The question of dependence, psychological or physiological, hangs on the matter of withdrawal symptoms; and here the committee argued that "the lack of persistent abstinence symptoms after withdrawal of alcohol was held to indicate the absence of dependence in a degree comparable to that produced by morphine-like substances."

Here the committee stubbed its collective toe, but no blame should attach. Quite understandably, its members concurred in a myth for which every one who has specialized in the treatment of alcoholism must share some responsibility. American and European medical journals abound with statements to the effect that the withdrawal of alcohol is never followed by serious symptoms. The myth has stood on two legs: there have been many alcoholics whose serious symptoms, such as delirium tremens, began while they were still drinking; and there have been even more alcoholics who, when their alcohol was withdrawn on admission to hospitals, experienced neither delirium nor convulsions.

It took Dr. Harris Isbell to convince us that the myth lacked truth. Dr. Isbell is the director of the Addiction Research Center in the Public Health Service Hospital at Lexington, Kentucky. Intrigued by reports of clinical findings which seemed at variance with the textbook axioms, he organized a carefully controlled experiment.

Ten men, from twenty-six to forty years old, in excellent physical condition, volunteered to drink alcohol in large doses over a long period of time. The men were all former morphine addicts; each had been psychiatrically diagnosed as having "character disorders" or "inadequate personalities," in connection with which Dr. Isbell noted that their personality aberrations were no more severe than those frequently observed in alcoholics.

Since the experiment was conducted in a closed ward of the Public Health Service Hospital, it was absolutely controlled. On a regular basis, the men were checked by physicians, psychiatrists, and laboratory technicians. The men were fed a high-protein diet and got vitamins in addition.

Throughout the day and night, they drank ninety-five per cent ethyl alcohol diluted with two parts of water or fruit juice. For the first week or so their dosage was fairly small; it was increased for seven of the men to the point where they were drinking as much as 496 cc's of alcohol daily (as diluted, this is equivalent to 1.5 quarts of sixty-three proof liquor, or one quart of ninety-five proof liquor diluted with a pint of water or fruit juice) or about as much as it is believed a man of average weight can metabolize in a day.

Three of the ten quit after seven to sixteen days of drinking. They had hangovers. A fourth quit after thirty-four days. He had a severe hangover. The other six drank for from forty-eight to eighty-seven days, during which each drank more than 400 cc's for at least forty-five days. None had convulsions or delirium so long as he continued to drink. When alcohol was withdrawn, all six had marked tremors, extreme weakness, profuse perspiration, nausea, vomiting, diarrhoea, elevated blood pressure, slight to marked fever, insomnia, and loss of appetite. Four had visual and auditory hallucinations, and two went into delirium, one so severely that he had to be given massive doses of barbiturates which were gradually withdrawn. One of the men had seven convulsions in the first thirty hours after withdrawal and was in such serious condition that he required medication with barbiturates for eighteen days. In this latter, most severe case, withdrawal symptoms continued for almost three months.

Now delirium and convulsions are dangerous symptoms. Delirium tremens is said to result in a mortality of from five to fifteen per cent. More simply stated, withdrawal of alcohol from a chronic alcoholic can result in death. In sharp contrast, however, the withdrawal symptoms of morphine are markedly uncomfortable but they do not include convulsions or delirium and, in uncomplicated cases, there is no danger of death.

Dr. Isbell's experiment persuades that the withdrawal symptoms of acute chronic alcoholism are more serious than those of morphinism.

To explain how so many clinicians could have reached an

opposite conclusion, he suggests that those alcoholics who, on admission to hospitals, experienced no serious withdrawal symptoms were like the first four of his ten to quit drinking: that is, their drinking bouts had not lasted long enough to warrant their having severe withdrawal symptoms. In the case of those who go into delirium tremens while still drinking, his hypothesis is that, although they are still drinking, they are drinking less, and so much less that their blood alcohol has dropped to the point where withdrawal symptoms could be expected. In this connection, he has written: "If a person who has been consuming 450 to 500 cc's of 95 per cent alcohol daily reduces his consumption to 390 to 440 cc's daily, the concentration of alcohol in his blood would fall to zero and withdrawal symptoms might develop in spite of the fact that he would still be consuming what is usually regarded as a very large amount of alcohol."

In any event, he has demonstrated that alcohol does produce withdrawal symptoms, and that they are severe.

To return, then, to the three criteria set up:

1. Alcohol does create, in those addicted to it, an overpowering desire or need to continue taking the drug, and many of them will seek to obtain it by any means;

2. Users of alcohol, while acquiring a tolerance to the drug, do not seem to acquire anything like the tolerance of morphine users;

3. Withdrawal of alcohol from heavy drinkers can result in symptoms more severe and more persistent than those caused by withdrawal of morphine and allied drugs.

This being the case, is alcohol a drug liable to produce addiction? Dr. Isbell, while criticizing the Expert Committee's comments about withdrawal symptoms, nevertheless agreed with the decision to place alcohol in a category of its own, somewhere between the addiction-producing and the habit-forming drugs.

Should it be so? Surely the controlling factor in removing alcohol from the category of addiction-producing drugs is the fact that so many of us are in the habit of relying on this drug for our social pleasures. And so, collectively, we refuse to stigmatize it. We will go so far as to formulate a definition which clearly stigmatizes it but then refuse to permit its inclusion under that definition.

We are prepared to agree that there are a few of us for whom alcohol is an addiction-producing drug. And we are prepared to take the further step of engaging to help those few. Our social ambivalence will permit us to go no further.

And so need help

In an astonishingly short time there has taken place what amounts to a revolution in our thinking about alcoholism, and the finest fruits of this revolution are the hopes that have been brought to every alcoholic, and to the family and friends of every alcoholic.

Quite probably all the fruits of this revolution are still to be harvested, but the tangible benefits achieved to this moment are resounding and far-reaching. Many factors, many people, many organizations can pridefully share the credit for having brought the revolution about, but there is no argument as to the three forces that have been most important. To list them in the order of their inception, they are:

The Laboratory of Applied Physiology of Yale University, where in 1930, under the direction of Dr. Howard Haggard, there was launched an intensive program of experiments with the physiology of alcohol. In time it was recognized that this approach was too limited, and the program was expanded as the Center of Alcohol Studies, involving sociology, psychiatry, psychology, economics, law, and medicine.

Alcoholics Anonymous, the remarkable fellowship of recovered alcoholics which, founded in 1935, has spread from this country across both oceans and now numbers an international membership of more than 200,000.

The National Committee on Alcoholism which, organized in the fall of 1944, has focused its energies in the areas of public education and community organization.

These three groups have been different things to different people, and have done many things of urgent importance, but their signal accomplishment has been to inspire a salutary change in the climate of our thinking. In its different way, each has perceived and argued that something had to be done and that something could be done for the alcoholic. The Yale Center has mobilized professional leaders, stimulated thought and action, and provided a clearing-house and an exchange for information, ideas, techniques. The National Committee has translated information and ideas to the general public, and spurred local communities into action. A.A., which is primarily a therapeutic approach, has been transformed into something even, if possible, more important: a shining example, a talking-point, a proof for alcoholics of all kinds, even those for whom A.A.'s therapeutic program does not work.

The results have been inestimable.

For the alcoholic, basically, needs only two things to effect a recovery from his addiction: he needs a degree of insight into his personal problems, and he needs the will to get well. Before there was general public acceptance of the concept that alcoholism is a disease, it was vastly more difficult for the alcoholic to gain any insight into his problems. Before he was provided with examples, he had less incentive and more despair, it was easier for him to rationalize his way into worse sickness, he was always more dangerously prone to relapse.

Today he is more likely to sense he needs help, and sooner than would have been the case ten years ago; certainly he comes better prepared to face his problems and get well. And when he comes for help he will find that society, too, is better prepared to help him.

I

Medical historians have dug up the fact that a British Navy physician, Thomas Trotter, in 1788 wrote a dissertation in Latin which was a few years later published in English as "Essay, Medical, Philosophical and Chemical, on Drunkenness." Many of the ancients had written briefly on the subject of excessive drinking, from a moral and philosophical standpoint; but, at least in western civilization, Trotter was the first medical man to call it a disease and discuss it in those terms. He wrote: "Are not habits of drunkenness more often produced by mental affections than corporeal diseases?" And again: "The seeds of this disease (the habit of inebriety), I suspect, like many others, are often sown in infancy. I do not merely allude to moral education." And again: "It is to be remembered that a bodily infirmity is not the only thing to be corrected. The habit of drunkenness is a disease of the mind. The soul itself has received impressions that are incompatible with its reasoning powers. The subject, in all respects, requires great address; and you must beware how you inveigh against the propensity; for the cravings of appetite for the poisonous draught are to the intemperate drinker as much the inclinations of nature, for the time, as a draught of cold water to a traveller panting with thirst in the desert."

Trotter's intuitive perceptions were not, understandably, followed up. One hundred and fifty years later it would still be difficult, despite the construction of a scientific basis for his observations, to persuade any considerable number of alcoholics or non-alcoholics that the ailment was psychogenic. In Europe, and especially in Switzerland, medical men had begun to treat alcoholism by the latter years of the nineteenth century, but in the United States the best that could be offered was the Keeley "cure," an ineffectual combination of aversion treatment and temporary seclusion.

It is noteworthy that the next efforts to cope with alcoholism were made by laymen. It would seem to be the case that the medical profession is not notably more progressive, even in matters that should concern them, than society in general. After the first World War some lay therapists—first in Boston and later in Philadelphia—undertook the task of recovering alcoholics. Their success was limited but significant. At least they were able to demonstrate that the job could be done. Nobody else, at least at this point, cared.

In the mid-1930's the aversion treatment was given a far more rigorous and exhaustive test. Out on the west coast, in two sanitoriums founded by Charles Shadel, alcoholics were given a course of treatment calculated to produce in them a conditioned reflex against alcohol. This is a psychiatric method based on the experiments of the Russian physiologist Pavlov. The purpose is to establish in the patient an aversion to the sight, smell, taste, or even the thought of alcoholic beverages. It is done by giving the patient emetine within a few minutes of his taking a drink: he will feel nauseous, and will vomit. An injection of emetine, a drink, vomit: the last two experiences are so connected, it is conjectured, as to set up in his mind an association that will satisfactorily reduce his desire to drink. The process must be repeated from four to six times within ten days, and it must thereafter be reinforced with later treatments during the first, and even a second, year. The psychiatrists at these sanitoriums screen applicants with some care, for they prefer to admit only those who demonstrate a strong will to recovery; informal psychotherapy is used as an adjunct to the conditioned-reflex treatment. According to a recent follow-up of some five thousand patients treated over a period of fourteen years, it is claimed that a little more than one out of every two have recovered—that is, have been abstinent for two years or longer.

But this was an almost wholly local attempt. In the main, alcoholics throughout the United States continued to be considered, by doctors and laity alike, as weak-willed, self-pampering, spineless drunks who were digging their own graves and should be permitted to continue doing so undisturbed.

It was also in the mid-1930's that Alcoholics Anonymous was born.

A.A.'s story is so familiar that, rather than retell it, we propose only to comment on it. At the outset, the founders groped toward what they wanted. They made the same mistake, at first, that every person working with an alcoholic has made: they preached. Doctors had too rarely helped them; priests and ministers had too rarely helped them; they felt they had to go it alone. They sensed that what was required of them was the building of a companionship among alcoholics that would give them something to do in their spare time; they were aware that if their fellowship was not to explode at once, controversial questions would have to be outlawed, for they knew better than most how low is the threshold of the alcoholic's tolerance for tension and frustration. So their group, they reasoned, must be non-sectarian, must be non-political, must abjure reform and steer clear of the Wet-Dry controversy. And it had to be open: "The only requirement for membership in A.A. is an honest desire to get over drinking."

But they felt, too, the need for some sort of positive program. How to formulate something that would be positive, and yet non-controversial? They had found the hard way that preaching was not enough, that something concrete had to be offered the alcoholic in exchange for his alcohol and his hours of drinking; and they knew the something concrete had to be more than a coffee-urn at their meetings so that coffee might be substituted for alcohol. Gradually the celebrated Twelve Steps were hammered out.

1. We admitted that we were powerless over alcohol—that our lives had become unmanageable.

2. Came to believe that a Power greater than ourselves could restore us to sanity.

3. Made a decision to turn our will and our lives over to the care of God *as we understood Him.*

4. Made a searching and fearless moral inventory of ourselves.

5. Admitted to God, to ourselves and to another human being the exact nature of our wrongs.

6. Were entirely ready to have God remove all these defects of character.

7. Humbly asked Him to remove our shortcomings.

8. Made a list of all persons we had harmed, and became willing to make amends to them all.

9. Made direct amends to such people wherever possible, except when to do so would injure them or others.

10. Continued to take personal inventory and when we were wrong, promptly admitted it.

11. Sought through prayer and meditation to improve our conscious contact with God *as we understood Him,* praying

only for knowledge of His will for us and the power to carry that out.

12. Having had a spiritual awakening as the result of these steps, we tried to carry this message to alcoholics and practice these principles in all our affairs.

Inherent in this program is a spiritual concept which has proven a barrier to many alcoholics and kept them out of A.A. There is no doubt that the men who framed the twelve steps had won their own way to sobriety by virtue of spiritual experiences. And yet members of A.A. insist that the spiritual emphasis should constitute no barrier. What is important is the recognition that there is some Power greater than oneself. They call attention to the italicized phrase *as we understood Him;* one A.A. member vigorously thumped a radiator: "It can be the steam in this radiator here, if you want," she said; "the point is you must recognize that there is something bigger and stronger and more powerful than you."

What is under attack, in at least three of the twelve steps, is the alcoholic's sense of omnipotence (or invulnerability, or grandiosity). It is the *sine qua non.* We admitted: we consented; we accepted; we recognized; we surrendered: the painful first step toward the realities of a hazardous existence in a real world, where one's own achievement is the proper yardstick by which to measure one's self-esteem.

And under attack, too, is the alcoholic's egocentricity, his exclusive and narcissistic self-concern. Not only must he retrace the past but he must consent to maintain an armed vigil in the present and future.

Meantime, in his weekly meetings, he is thrust into a social milieu. The fearful loneliness he experienced, in a bar or in his room, withdrawn from family and friends, gradually cut off from every interest except that of his addiction, is now counterposed by a circle of people—strangers at first, then acquaintances, then friends and firm associates—whom he can trust in his conviction of their similar, identical, or shared experiences. He can switch his dependency to this group; but if he does, it is likely that he will soon learn, instead, a more fulfilling interdependence as he works with one or two others of his group in helping to recover still another alcoholic.

And in his meetings, it is likely that he will achieve a measure of serenity. His fellow-members are aware that fractious, nettlesome subjects spawn anger, resentment, and tension; "an alcoholic plus a resentment equals a drunk," they say, "as surely as two plus two equals four," and they wisely temper their tones of voice and blunt their sharp arguments.

There is, moreover, in A.A.'s closed meetings, what amounts to a kind of informal group psychotherapy. Certainly, in the give-and-take, in the exchange of common experiences, the A.A. member has ample opportunity to gain a better insight into the nature of his personal problems.

However the program is interpreted, there is no doubt that it has succeeded. And its success has led many a psychiatrist to examine and analyze, seeking how he can learn to be of more help to his alcoholic patients whether or not they are A.A. members. Quite often his patients are also A.A. members, for the realization has grown that A.A., while supremely well geared to help the alcoholic control his symptom, his drinking, cannot be expected to get at the deep-rooted neurosis.

How can this best be done?

We live in the age of chemotherapy. One after another, diseases have been mastered by one or another of the sulfa drugs or the antibiotics or the steroids. It is natural that those sick of alcoholism should yearn for their wonder drug, their pill which would so easily quell the sickness, bring health and happiness. And, indeed, explorations have been conducted along these physiological avenues. One of the most promising, for a time, seemed to indicate that perhaps a metabolic disturbance was the cause of alcoholism.

But those who consider alcoholism chiefly as a metabolic disturbance are confusing the effects of prolonged drinking with the cause. There is no doubt that the alcoholic, by the time he arrives for treatment, may be a badly depleted individual. Certainly he can never get over his addiction without paying due attention to the demands of his physical constitution. He may have been living for days on whisky, a substance which has no minerals, no vitamins, no proteins, and none of the essential fats. In addition he may have been squandering his physical reserves through lack of sleep and through manic-like activity. Feeling no pain, he may have sustained physical injuries, sometimes serious ones; and he has certainly run the gamut of emotions. Of course his adrenal is depleted, but so is every other cell in his body. Emotionally and physically he is in a state equivalent to a decompensation, and in the post-alcoholic state of hangover he should be given everything he lacks. This may occasionally mean adrenal cortical extract; but surely it does mean salt, vitamins, food, mild or heavy sedation, Thorazine for his anxiety and for his devastating tremors. In any case, and most importantly, he will need reassurance that he can recover.

Even when an alcoholic is in a free interval—that is, when he is not drinking—his routine is likely to be unhealthy. Frequently he lives alone, and it usually follows that his diet is inadequate. Even if he is so fortunate as to be living with his family he may eat erratically. Glucose tolerance tests sometimes reveal low blood sugar levels; this will lead to such symptoms of hypoglycemia as fatigue, apathy, and a loss of zest for working or even for living. The alcoholic may have tried to counteract this by drinking astonishing amounts of coffee, Coca-Cola, or other sweet drinks, with the result that his blood-sugar levels will continue to fluctuate abnormally. Since he has learned to use alcohol for every type of discomfort, it is natural for him to turn, sooner or later, back to alcohol as the most quickly absorbed form of carbohydrate, in order to throw off his lassitude. His sleep pattern is often badly disturbed, for not only must he fight against his neurotic self but he must also overcome the stimulating effects of the coffee, the Coca-Cola, or the Dexedrine. It is not uncommon for an alcoholic to drink, in a free interval, as much as twenty cups of coffee in a day; some have been known to drink fifty cups in a day.

So his deranged physiology must be rectified, as a first step in his rehabilitation. He needs a high protein diet. Three square meals a day, together with interval feedings of some sort of palatable, balanced combination of powdered milk and yeast proteins, minerals, vitamins, and nucleic acid will bring dramatic improvement in his sense of well-being. As for adrenal cortical extract, while it *may* occasionally help during the hangover period, it is of no value in combating the addiction.

It is the unfortunate fact that, at least at the present stage of our knowledge, chemotherapy offers no possible solution for alcoholism. There is no pill, no wonder drug that will undo the damage done by a neurosis to a personality structure. There is no easy path. Growing up is, under the most wholesome conditions, hard and painful work; overcoming a neurosis is even harder and more painful. For in the process one must relive, re-experience, lay bare emotions that have been carefully and necessarily hidden, discover why it was necessary to hide them, and, going on from strength to strength, arrive finally at the time when the distorting, crippling, nightmare fantasies of the buried past have been exhumed, faced, recognized as only bugbears, fitted into their proper perspective, and filed away again

—this time not in the unconscious, where they would continue to do damage, but in the preconscious, where they can be safely ignored. The process has been described as a kind of re-education, but in fact it is a more profound and more arduous education. It is, for the neurotic, the only present answer. It is psychotherapy.

Psychotherapy is of various kinds, and this is fortunate, for so are alcoholics, and there are practical as well as theoretical considerations that govern the choice of therapy to fit the individual. There is psychoanalysis, there is psychiatric counseling, there is lay therapy conducted by a recovered alcoholic, there is psychiatry, there is group psychotherapy, there is hypnoanalysis, and there is psychodrama or play therapy. The therapists may work in a sanatorium, a prison, an out-patient clinic, or a doctor's office. All these have been used, and more often than not combinations of two or more of them have been used for the same patient. In the broadest sense of the term, psychotherapy begins with the very first interview, whether it be with a receptionist, a social worker, or a doctor and whether the patient is drunk, in the depths of a hangover, or in a free interval. One takes the cue from the patient, responding to each of these phases of the illness differently but at all times in a friendly way. If there was ever a vicious circle, alcoholism is one: the doctor, faced with an alcoholic patient for the first time, must tax his ingenuity to the utmost to find where, when, and how to break in on the circle. He learns he must break in wherever the patient allows it, and if that moment arrives when the patient is drunk and disrupting office procedures and schedules, so much the worse, but the moment must be seized.

Under ideal conditions, analysis would always be the psychotherapy of choice. Only analysts have been trained in the specific and complex problems of psychodynamics; only analysts, it must be insisted, have been thoroughly educated in the theory of neuroses, their etiology and their therapy. Nevertheless, there are reasons why analysis is not always the best treatment for an alcoholic.

In the first place, the average alcoholic finds it difficult enough to recognize that he has a problem with liquor. Having arrived at that point, he is likely to be convinced that alcohol is his only problem: to help him get dry and stay dry is all he wants from any doctor. But before analysis will be of any use to him, he must have taken a further step: he must have recognized that he is neurotic, that the alcohol is only a symptom; he must be prepared to enter on a course of therapy that may extend over years.

And during that time he must stay sober. Analysis demands of him his attention and his will; the nature of the treatment requires of him that he obey the basic rule of saying everything that comes into his mind, without selection. A sodden drunk will, to say the least, find it difficult to obey this rule, and even if able to associate will find it impossible to profit from the technique. Nor will it be easy for him to give up his drinking during analysis. For the drug is ego-syntonic, that is, it is pleasurable, it gratifies the ego. In every analysis the common foe against which, as allies, the doctor and the patient fight is the patient's resistance. His resistance may show up in any of a thousand ways, from his arriving five minutes late for his appointment to his lying mute on the couch for ten or fifteen or fifty minutes at a time. The overcoming of resistance is a thorny thing. The alcoholic will always be tempted to drink again, as his own additional and characteristic form of resistance.

Moreover, under the best of circumstances the analysis of an alcoholic is doubly difficult because the origin of his neurosis is so archaic in terms of his ego development. His problem reaches back to his infancy. Layer after layer must be stripped

173

away. The process is bound to be a severe test of his ability to tolerate tension.

Finally, there is the practical consideration of expense. The alcoholic, if he has been severely addicted, is likely to have no money. In any event his earning power will at best be problematical. And any course of therapy that extends over as long a period as analysis is expensive.

In the face of these very real difficulties, analysis remains the best method of tackling the alcoholic neurosis. Fortunately, if the patient has a real will to get well, modern medicine has contributed a chemical compound which can, of itself, cancel out one of the difficulties, that of staying sober. This compound is called Antabuse.*

In Denmark, several years ago, it was accidentally discovered that the organic compound tetraethylthiuram disulfide had the peculiar property of making anyone who took it sensitive to alcohol. Since then it has been used in the treatment of alcohol addiction in many thousands of cases throughout Europe, Canada, and the United States. After medication with this compound, even a small drink of alcohol will result in flushing of the face, palpitation, difficulty in breathing, a pounding headache, a sense of apprehension, and frequently nausea and vomiting. There may, in addition, be an abrupt fall of the systolic blood pressure very like that occurring in surgical shock. The severity of the reaction depends on the dosage of Antabuse, the amount of alcohol drunk, and the individual. After an hour or two the patient falls asleep to awake refreshed two or three hours later.

Precisely how and why this happens is still unknown. This much is known: the Antabuse blocks some enzyme system in

* One of the present authors, Dr. Fox, has had occasion to give Antabuse to more than eight hundred patients over the past six years. The discussion of the drug in these pages is based on her experience.

the liver and thereby interferes with the metabolism of acetaldehyde, which is one of the intermediate products of the combustion of alcohol in the body. The toxic effects of the Antabuse result from the accumulation of this acetaldehyde.

The drug is not dangerous. Anybody can take it so long as he understands what he is taking and realizes that if he drinks alcohol on top of it he may get seriously sick. Some caution should be exercised in the case of elderly people with a hypertension or evidence of some cardiovascular disease, but this is not because Antabuse is toxic for them but only because experimentation on their part with alcohol might result in cardiac failure.

When Antabuse was first introduced into this country, it was felt necessary to give each patient a test dose of alcohol in the hospital so that he would have a clear idea of the results of experimentation with drinking. But gradually this practice has been dropped as unnecessary.

How efficacious is Antabuse? As with any method of treating alcoholism, the results depend on the measure of the individual's will to get well. Antabuse alone can cure very few if any cases of alcoholism; taken in conjunction with psychotherapy, it can be of very real use. Indeed, it should be used only as an adjunct to psychotherapy, and its prescription might well be limited to those physicians who are prepared to give each patient the many hours and painstaking attention he will need to recover from his addiction.

This is what Antabuse helps to accomplish:

It gives the individual an external control. It prevents impulsive drinking. If he is waylaid, on a Monday afternoon, by boredom or by anxiety or by annoyance or by a feeling of rejection, he nevertheless knows that he must wait until Saturday before he can safely take a drink—and by that time he will have been able to find some other way of controlling his frustration. Then too, when one is taking Antabuse, his pre-occupation with alcohol disappears. If he is not taking the drug, he may be faced a hundred times a day with the decision to drink or not to drink; but with Antabuse there can be only one decision: it can become as routine a habit pattern as brushing one's teeth in the morning. And once that one decision has been made, sobriety will, he knows, follow that day and for the next five days thereafter.

Is it a crutch? Well, yes, perhaps; but so what? Aspirin is a crutch against a headache; insulin is a crutch for the diabetic; and what, after all, is wrong with a crutch? Ask the man whose leg has been broken. Indeed, friendship is a crutch, and so is Alcoholics Anonymous, and so can be love.

For many alcoholics, the first Antabuse pill means tremendous relief: it is a positive step, so long as the individual regards it as something friendly, helpful, rather like a compassionate mother who is assisting him in his resolve not to drink. The danger arises when the individual looks on the drug as something hostile and forbidding, and equates it emotionally with a harsh, restrictive parent. In such a case, the alcoholic will call on his fertile imagination to supply him with a dozen reasons against taking the pill, or, having taken it, will find nearly as many to deceive the person who has given it to him. Thus, he may hold it under his tongue and spit it out later; or switch the pills in the bottle so that in fact he is taking only aspirin when he seems to be taking Antabuse; or he will swallow the pill, wait for the giver to leave, and then put his finger down his throat and vomit the pill back up.

In such cases, it is not only unwise, it is impossible to force Antabuse on the alcoholic. ("Don't make me submit again!") It is, typically, unwise to give the pills to the alcoholic's mother or wife, asking her in turn to give them to the patient. For no matter how adroitly or understandingly she may offer it, the gesture, coming from her, may arouse his resentment.

But properly administered, Antabuse is a splendid beachhead for the alcoholic's war against alcohol. The man or woman taking it for the first time may be concerned: Is it dangerous? Four years ago a man, formerly a judge, who was at the time seventy-seven years old and who had had a coronary occlusion one month before seeking help for his alcoholism, took his first dose of Antabuse. He has taken some routinely every day since then. Now eighty-one, he is writing his memoirs and even undertaking to perform legal services for a few clients. Without the Antabuse, there can be no question that alcohol would have killed him.

What will happen if one takes it over a period of several years? Nothing but good. Maggie T is a waitress who has been taking Antabuse regularly for six years. Prior to that, she was forced to keep her child in foster-homes; she rarely had enough money to pay for his keep. But since she has been taking the drug, her work has been steady (she serves alcoholic drinks along with the meals she brings her customers), her anxiety attacks have been less frequent and less severe, and, most important, her son has been living at home with her. Edward G has likewise been taking Antabuse for the past six years. When he started, he was on the Bowery, a derelict, unemployed and long separated from his wife. Since the day, six years ago, when he took his first pill, his path has reached steadily upward. He found a job first as an elevator man; earned enough to buy himself a decent suit of clothes; searched for and located his wife and children; found himself a job back in his profession; was at length promoted and then transferred to the Washington bureau of his newspaper. He still takes one quarter of a pill twice a week.

These things have happened because Antabuse enables the alcoholic to achieve sobriety long enough so that his habit patterns will change, and long enough so that psychotherapy can be instituted. Of course, the drug is not always able to effect such salutary transformations. Typically, during the first few weeks on Antabuse the alcoholic is enthusiastic, happy to be taking it. After perhaps two months, he may decide that he was never an alcoholic but only a social drinker, stop the Antabuse, and find to his dismay that he is back where he started. Or, after the same two or three months, he may get angry with the drug, and quite deliberately stop taking it and go off on a bender. Or, at about the same time, he may feel so secure, so filled with self-esteem and self-righteousness, that he may decide he's had it; two months, he may feel, is long enough. Soon after, however, he is likely to find himself in a difficult situation, a situation in which, beckoned by his unconscious, he will take a drink—for now he will be without his protection.

And so, on the basis of these and other experiences, it seems wise and expedient to recommend that Antabuse be routinely taken for about two years, if completely new and different habit patterns are to be insured.

Certainly the analysis of alcoholics can be greatly helped by the use of Antabuse. The patient's willingness to take the drug can even constitute a measure of his sincerity. Alcohol is a powerful adversary, especially during the early days of an analysis, when the drinking problem itself is being tackled: the alcoholic's ego strength is low; he needs a lot of support. He may be able to find it if there is a strong transference relationship; in any event, Antabuse will protect him.

But if every analyst in the country were to devote himself exclusively to alcoholic patients, there would still be a grievously large number of these sick people requiring attention. And so they must gain their insights into their difficulties with the help of other forms of psychotherapy. Of these other forms, psychiatric counseling and group therapy are probably the best.

Psychiatric counseling is predicated on the firm kindness and sympathy of a physician. To the alcoholic, who has alternately been scolded and threatened, misunderstood, and given uncomprehending variations of the carrot-and-club treatment, a psychiatrist's interest, regard, sympathy, and understanding are therapeutic in themselves. Moreover, counseling offers the alcoholic the opportunity to talk about his problems, to see the things that concern him as specific ideas clothed in words rather than as nameless, formless, emotional dreads. As he comes to understand that his overpowering emotions are something that the doctor obviously understands on the basis of experience with other patients, the alcoholic gains confidence in his ability to surmount them, master them, control them. Sound counseling can go far in helping a man get insight. And insight, as we have said, together with the will to get well, is considerably more than half the battle.

Group therapy is, for many alcoholics, an even better method, for here the individual is one of eight or ten people suffering from the same malady. The experience of every group therapist is the same: he finds that the members of a group gain in understanding of their own problems by seeing how the same problems afflict others. Usually, indeed, the members of a group will make the kind of penetrating and incisive comment to one of their number, and make it be helpful, better than can the therapist himself. Additionally, group therapy has the advantage of helping the alcoholic become socialized, in much the same fashion that A.A. has done. But group therapy on a formal basis can, because it is under the guidance of a trained therapist, often do more in helping the severely neurotic alcoholic come to grips with his neurosis than can an A.A. meeting.

It is often the case that the alcoholic—or his family—is aware how much he needs help but simply has no idea of where to turn to get it. It should be urged that, in the larger cities at least, every clergyman knows where and when the nearest chapter of A.A. meets, knows how to get in touch with an A.A. member, and thus can steer the alcoholic—or a member of his family—in the direction of help. Likewise, many doctors today cooperate with A.A., just as, in turn, A.A. increasingly urges some of its members to seek specific medical assistance, as required. In many towns and cities, A.A.'s telephone number is given a prominent position in the phone book.

Whatever the choice of psychotherapy, the treatment of an alcoholic involves a long and complicated process of rehabilitation. Only in exceptional circumstances can the psychotherapist accomplish the job alone. Typically, he will need the help of a team: psychologists, social workers, nurses, experts in vocational guidance and recreation, hospitals and rest homes, schools, colleges, courts, churches, social and fraternal organizations, A.A.—in fact, all that our complex society has to offer. It is in virtue of this kind of teamwork that modern medicine has been able to push the rate of recovery from alcoholism up: up from thirty per cent ten or twelve years ago to fifty to sixty per cent today.

The absolute necessity of this kind of teamwork has been underlined, too, as specialists in the field of alcoholism have come to recognize one of the most stubborn opponents of the alcoholic's recovery—his own family.

II

It is not necessarily true that an alcoholic's wife acts in such a way as to cause him to drink. But it is often at least partly the case.

It is not necessarily true that an alcoholic unconsciously seeks out and marries the kind of woman who will complement his neurotic tendency to drink excessively and addictively. But it is often at least partly the case.

It is not necessarily true that the alcoholic who has never married has not because his neurotic needs have been satisfactorily met by a mother, or an older sister. But it is often at least partly the case.

It is not necessarily true that a woman, to fulfill her own unconscious needs, will seek out and marry the kind of neurotic whose underlying character traits mark him as prone to become an alcoholic. But this, too, is often at least partly the case, just as it is partly the case that such a woman will, after the marriage ceremony, behave in such a way as to nurse her husband's underlying character traits into full and riotous command over him.*

This much is necessarily true: The alcoholic cannot be successfully treated and his recovery effected without the firm, sympathetic, and understanding cooperation of his wife or family. Indeed, since to effect his recovery will involve deep and far-reaching changes not only in his way of life but in his personality, it may be that his wife, if she wishes to save her marriage, may have to undertake psychotherapy herself, for herself. This should not be hard to understand. We choose a husband or wife for what seem to us to be quite conscious reasons but there are unconscious factors very much at work too. It happens often enough for it to have been a matter of common observation by many psychiatrists that a woman whose father was an alcoholic will marry a man who becomes an alcoholic. Obviously such a woman did not say to herself:

* Throughout this discussion, as elsewhere, for the sake of convenience, we are talking about the alcoholic as though he were always masculine. The alcoholic may, of course, be a woman.

"I'll marry Bill because he drinks too much too often, just the way Daddy did!" But unconsciously she did respond to qualities in Bill which were strikingly similar to qualities in the father whom she had loved, respected, and cared for (or feared and hated but nonetheless was drawn to). But the qualities in her husband that governed her unconscious selection of him will undergo a change if, in the process of his recovery from alcoholism, he undertakes thorough psychotherapy. She will, therefore, unconsciously rebel against these changes and fight the therapy that is helping him. What is neurotic in her drew her to him: what is neurotic in her will resist change in him. If her marriage is to be saved, and if her husband is to recover from his alcoholism, she must understand (just as he has done) that she must seek help, psychotherapeutic help.

As it happens, Alcoholics Anonymous quickly became aware of how serious a problem was posed by the alcoholic's family. The A.A. solution has been sound and pragmatic, even if it is not addressed to the wife's deeper psychological needs. Their solution has been to form A.A. auxiliaries, usually called Al-Anon Family Groups. Here wives of alcoholics who are not A.A. members may meet with wives of men who have only recently joined A.A., or who are married to men who have been in A.A. for five or ten years. Here they can discuss the continuing problem posed by the cumulative crisis in their lives. Here they may meet a woman who will smilingly tell how she exploded in a temper tantrum when her husband asked if she was ready to go to the weekly Sunday night meeting; how she burst out with "Darn your old meeting!" and threw a shoe at him; and how she came to realize that if the twelve steps were good for him they might be good for her as well. Actually, A.A. has recognized that the recovered alcoholic may grow away from his wife in just the fashion outlined earlier. And their recommendation that alcoholics' wives likewise take the twelve steps is, in a sense, a recommendation that the wives undertake an informal program of self-therapy.

Just as there is no single alcoholic personality, so there is no single pattern of obstruction by the wife or family to the alcoholic's treatment or recovery. Sometimes the wife may be the protective, maternal kind of woman who marries a man whom she knows to be an alcoholic, in order to, as she thinks, help him over his addiction. But unconsciously she wants no part of his recovery. Her need is to dominate a weaker man; his recovery is an actual threat to her neurotic demand that he be weak, inferior, helpless, dependent. It is not unusual to meet a woman who has been married to more than one alcoholic. One woman whose husband applied for treatment remarked, during the course of an interview, that she had been married four times; each of her husbands had been an alcoholic; so had her father.*

And there are women who choose to suffer. Pleasure in pain has always its two sides: just as this kind of woman derives pleasure from the painful situation of being married to an alcoholic, so she also derives pleasure from the pain she is able to inflict by precipitating the argument, the quarrel, the tension which unconsciously she knows will land her husband in another drinking bout, inevitably followed by his dreadful remorse and self-reproach.†

* Dr. Samuel Futterman, a psychiatrist practicing in Beverly Hills, California, has reported a similar instance, that of a wife who "stated that she saw no use in divorcing her third husband because of his drinking because she knew she would only marry another alcoholic."
† Thelma Whalen, an executive in a Dallas, Texas, Family Service Agency, has, on the basis of her considerable day-to-day experience with the wives of alcoholics, devised a handy rule-of-thumb by which she categorizes them. There is Suffering Susan, whose "need to punish herself is the dominating characteristic which forms the nucleus of her personality." There is Controlling Catherine, who "knew all about [her hus-

Perhaps the greatest barrier a loving wife or family can erect in the way of an alcoholic's recovery has to do with his dependency pattern. We have already mentioned Richard W, whose dependency on his wife (whom he married quite obviously because she was the kind of woman she was—a mother substitute) is so great that he resents her leaving him alone even for a shopping trip. What can she do, to help her husband? What if she were to tell him that she was going to leave him? That she was going to divorce him, since she loved him too much to permit him to use her as he has done for the twelve years they have been married? If she were to do such a thing, it would constitute a truly terrible threat to his neurotic dependency. He would be devastated. He would implore her to stay. If her purpose was fixed, if she showed that she actually meant to leave, he might threaten her with frightening consequences, perhaps that he would kill himself were she to leave. Quite possibly he might get out a gun, put the muzzle to his temple, his face working with anguish. What is she to do? She loves him: she will be dreadfully afraid that he *will* kill himself if she leaves: and so she will stay. And W's infantile triumph will have taught him that he will always be able to get what he wants by such trumpery.

Wives of course have left their dependent husbands, and will again. It is a grievous wrench for both. Nor is it the only solution. The wives of the Richard W's can fight the de-

band's] drinking but knew things would be different once he had her to look out for him." (She might as easily have been nicknamed Domineering Dorothy.) There is Wavering Winifred, who is by turns furious and patient, fearful and competent, ruthless and tolerant—and who constantly teeters on the brink of a critical decision: should she leave her husband, or stay with him? Finally, there is Punitive Polly, who is "rivalrous, aggressive, and envious," no homebody, often older than her husband, often a career woman who earns more than her husband, "whose relationship to her husband resembles that of a boa constrictor to a rabbit."

pendency pattern right in their own homes, if they know how. But how are they to learn? Their need to respond to their husbands' dependency is as ingrained as the dependency itself. They can only succeed if they seek and get psychiatric help.

Too often they do not. Too often they remain protective, insisting that the husband's drinking problems are not his fault. Or, if they come to a doctor, seeking help for their husband, they are resentful when they are tendered the advice that they should themselves get psychotherapy. "Me? There's nothing wrong with *me!* It's my husband who has the drinking problem!" But it may be the wife who makes sure the drinking problem remains insoluble.

Marriage to an alcoholic is, under the best of circumstances, a stormy affair. A Seattle investigator * who has for three years been an active participant in an A.A. auxiliary with a fluctuating membership of about fifty wives, has formulated, on the basis of many discussions, a description of the continuing and cumulative crisis caused the family by an alcoholic husband. She reported only the broad similarities. She perceived seven stages:

At first there are attempts to deny the problem. The wife reproaches, but later feels guilty: has she not perhaps exaggerated? Is it any of her business? She had better forget it.

Then there are attempts to cover up. She lies to the employer, she fibs to the children, she is increasingly isolated from friends and increasingly resentful of her husband. Quarrels multiply. She tries threats, she hides his liquor, she tries to control his pocket money. She begins to feel terribly inadequate as a wife and as a person. And she begins to console herself with self-pity.

* Joan K. Jackson, who is a research fellow with the Department of Psychiatry of the University of Washington School of Medicine.

Now she nags increasingly, or retreats into extended periods of silence. The children, increasingly disturbed, become "tools in the struggle between father and mother." Sexual relations deteriorate. Her husband accuses her of rejecting him, or of being frigid. She is dismayed. The marriage is wholly disorganized. Her dominant emotion is fear: fear that he will beat her up, fear of what is happening to her children, fear of her own sanity.

She may now decide to take over all family responsibilities. If she is so fortunate as to have gotten in touch with A.A. members, she will begin to feel better about her fears. On the other hand, her self-reliance and assumption of the role of father as well as mother may aggravate his behavior: he may become more violent or may withdraw, more sullen.

In the fifth stage, she leaves him. Her decision may flow from some immediate and catastrophic quarrel or simply from accumulated tension.

Thereafter she tries to reorganize the family unit without him but, typically, he makes this difficult by repeated and drunken attempts to force himself back into the family.

If there is a seventh stage, it comes about only on the basis of his sobriety and his first steps toward recovery from his addiction. It is a shaky time, for can she be sure of his recovery? The reorganization of the family unit will at best be difficult.*

* In some ways, the period of rehabilitation is more difficult than any period of the alcoholic addiction. The term "dry drunk" has come into use to describe the period of sobriety during which an alcoholic is attempting to control his emotions, his hostilities, his aggressions, his impatience, his irritability. His tension and his tendency to depression during this period lead most often to a desire to avoid people, any people, no matter who they are or how close to him. During such a dry drunk, the best-intentioned behavior of a wife may well be intolerable to the alcoholic (or vice versa, if the alcoholic is a woman). During such a dry drunk, the best recourse for the alcoholic is attendance at A.A. meetings or reliance on fellow A.A. members between meetings.

These seven stages are generalized. The individual bumps in the road have been smoothed over, the personal hairpin turns straightened out. No story is like another, and this one can only be said to share features with the many individual stories of heartbreak. And in those individual stories, what part did the alcoholic's family play in interfering with his recovery? There is no way of knowing. But the experience with the families of alcoholics had by psychiatric social workers, nurses, and doctors would indicate that it is considerable.

It may be small comfort to the wife who today is trying to patch together a shattered life, but the fact is that, typically, her chances of redeeming her family and resurrecting her love for her husband and his for her are generally far better today than would have been the case even a scant ten years ago.

For our society as a whole is more genuinely understanding of the alcoholic's problem.

III

The National Committee on Alcoholism held its tenth annual meeting in March of 1955, and took the occasion to reflect on the changes that had been worked in the ten years of its existence.

Ten years ago, there were no voluntary agencies devoted to alcoholism. Today there are fifty-six local committees in twenty-seven states, Hawaii, Canada, Bermuda, and abroad.

Ten years ago, there were no alcoholism information centers. Today there are fifty-two such centers in the United States which have given information and help to an estimated one hundred thousand people.

Ten years ago, only ninety-six general hospitals accepted acute cases of alcoholism for treatment, and only one of these did so willingly. Today over three thousand general hospitals routinely accept acute cases.

Ten years ago two experimental clinics for diagnosis and treatment of alcoholism had just been opened under the aegis of the Yale Center. They were the first in the country. Today there are nearly one hundred out-patient clinics functioning in the United States.*

Ten years ago no state government had a program dealing with alcoholism. Today there are thirty-one state programs functioning; another three states have study programs in operation; another seven are considering legislation.

Ten years ago no industry admitted it had any problem connected with alcoholism. Today at least fifteen large corporations have either established programs of diagnosis and treatment within their organization, or support and cooperate with community programs.

Exciting though such a chart of achievement is, it presents only a partial picture. For the change that has come cannot always be set down in brief factual statements. For example: how many police court magistrates were there ten years ago who were prepared to take a humane, wise, and tolerant view of the repeater drunk, trembling with the shakes, hauled up before the majesty of the law for perhaps the twelfth time? There were, to be sure, a few; just as today there are still many whose disposition of the drunk is summary and callous. But a change has come, and it will affect more and more of the magistrates whose duty it is to handle the drunken offenders against society.

Typical of the change is what has happened in New York City. Magistrate Anna Kross (later to become Commissioner of Correction), dismayed by the number of cases involving

* For the most recent available list of out-patient clinics functioning in the United States, see the Appendix, page 195.

188

wife and husband as plaintiff and defendant, concerned as to what would happen to family and children should justice be dispensed in too cavalier a fashion, succeeded finally in establishing in New York City a unique court, the Home Term Court. Here the psychiatric social worker and the probation officer became figures of meaning and authority; the aim of the court was not to punish the wrong-doer, but to see how much could be done to effect a reconciliation, to bandage a wound, to save a marriage. As it became more and more abundantly clear how considerable a role was played by alcohol in the husband-wife fights that erupted only to land the participants in the Home Term Court, an alcoholism clinic was set up, to function as a regular and routine procedural part of the court. A clinical psychologist may be sitting in on the cases as they come before the judge, not in an ordinary court-room but in a room where all sit around a table to discuss a problem. The judge, with the advice of the psychologist, may decide to refer husband, or wife, or both, to the clinic for treatment. At any given time there are usually about one hundred cases being handled by this clinic; most of them are alcoholics, but a few are the wives or husbands of alcoholics. So soon as they are received by the clinic, there is a change in atmosphere: now there is no longer any question of punishment, now there is only an attitude of helpfulness and understanding.

And as in New York City, so throughout the country. To be sure, a clinic like that functioning in conjunction with New York City's Home Term Court is exceptional; but it is by no means exceptional for magistrates and judges in every large city to cooperate closely with units of Alcoholics Anonymous. There are A.A. chapters in most of our large penal institutions; prison doctors and priests or ministers have been swift to see how much good could come of such chapters;

and, rather more slowly, the committing judges have begun to appreciate how much better (and cheaper, too) is prophylaxis than belated treatment.

Industrial leaders have been moved, quite naturally, by more practical considerations. When a corporation hires a man to perform a skilled job, necessarily he must be trained for a time. This time is money, money that can be totted up on a balance sheet. There is an investment in such a worker, and perceptive business leaders like to protect their investments. But what if such a worker, after years of training and promotion to a position of some responsibility, begins to show a pattern of absenteeism, low output, error, accident proneness, disregard of safety, excessive waste? Should he be summarily fired? A few years ago the answer would have been a peremptory *yes;* still today the answer is *yes* more often than not. But increasingly personnel executives are beginning to wonder. Why fire the man in whom the company has such a considerable investment? Might it not in the long run be more economical to investigate, find out why the white-collar man is not performing his stint? why the machinist's output is so much lower?

The Yale Center, which has done so much to bring the problems of alcohol before society and force their inspection, calls such a man the half-man. He is, they urge, completely on the job, say, Thursday and Friday; on Friday he gets his pay-check; over Saturday and Sunday he fills his skin with alcohol; and on Monday he is absent "sick" and on Tuesday and even Wednesday, back at work, he will be below par. His attention will be riveted on the water-cooler, the men's room, the aspirin bottle in his desk-drawer, and the clock on the wall. Industry, then, has got from him two full days of work a week and maybe two half-days in addition. Can industry take the trouble to investigate, determine how many such half-men are on the payroll, and then decide whether or not it might be feasible and practical and even remunerative to set up a program of helping their problem-drinker employees?

The more far-sighted business leaders already have. Consolidated Edison, Standard Oil of New Jersey, Metropolitan Life, Allis-Chalmers, Du Pont, to list just a few of the bluer-chip concerns, have interested themselves in protecting their investment in their employees. The awareness grows that the half-man may turn out to be a member of the board of directors as easily as he may be a working stiff punching a time card.

Moreover, the unions involved may have been suspicious at first, the foremen who must cooperate by urging the half-man worker to take advantage of this newly instituted medical program may have been hostile when they were first approached, but increasingly there is nothing but enthusiasm, on every level. It is part of the changing climate. When the man who has said, "It's none of your business," or "All my buddies drink," or "I got a lot of troubles," or "Haven't been feeling so good," or "I can't stop," or something considerably ruder comes to the point where he can say, "I see. I'm sick. Okay, I'll give it a try," then a victory of no little importance for society has been won.

And, of course, it helps when management is able to say to a recalcitrant worker: "Take your choice. Be fired and stripped of all your pension and retirement rights, or get right over to that alcoholism clinic and save your job and your seniority and your pension." In an era when workers have won very considerable pension rights and retirement benefits, even the most recalcitrant worker will wonder if perhaps he should not indeed get over to that alcoholism clinic.

But the most dramatic evidence of the change in the climate of our thinking about alcoholism lies in what has been done by the legislatures of the several states. The picture is spotty and uneven. There are some states which—while forward-looking in regard to other matters—have been shamefully laggard about alcoholism (Illinois, Ohio, and Texas are perhaps the most obvious examples). But taken in its perspective the result to the moment is most heartening.

Thanks to the Yale Center, Connecticut led the way and is in many respects still the leader. It is now ten years since the Connecticut Commission on Alcoholism was established as an official state agency, supported by public funds. The Commission administers a fifty-bed hospital at Hartford and five full-time out-patient clinics in various parts of the state. Any resident of the state concerned with or affected by problems of alcoholism is eligible for the Commission's services, and no patient is turned away because he is broke. In its last annual report, the Commission was able to point to more than one thousand patients cared for in the hospital and more than one thousand, three hundred patients treated in the clinics.

In the last ten years more than $9,000,000 has been appropriated by twenty-seven states and the District of Columbia to operate alcoholism agencies; the amount for fiscal 1954 was $2,600,000. These funds, among other things, paid to care for a case-load of more than forty-four thousand alcoholic patients, for research programs in fourteen of the states, and for public information and education.

Perhaps, compared with the $10 billion we annually spend on liquor, a figure like $2.6 million seems trivial as the amount of public funds spent to fight the problems posed by liquor. But drop in the bucket though it may be, it will be followed by other, and larger, drops. The beginning has been made. The responsibility has been assumed.

It is a social responsibility, for only so can the moral stigma be removed from alcoholism and the disease recognized as a disease, only so can there be proper research and therapy. The causes of the disease are deeply rooted in society as a whole. In the United States today the pressures which work to produce alcoholism are uniquely social pressures.

And so the solution for the problems of alcoholism, when it comes, will be brought about thanks to a still greater assumption by society of its responsibility.

IV

It remains only to say a few words about whether alcoholism can be cured.

On every side, alcoholism is described as an incurable disease. Even the recovered alcoholic is by most people considered still to be sick, or at least different from the rest of us, in the sense that he cannot and can never resume ordinary, social, controlled drinking.

Some doctors have claimed that a few, a very few individuals—once clearly alcoholics—have been able to resume controlled drinking. They are so few as to be inconsiderable. (We have been able to turn up only two cases, and in each of these there were circumstances that tend to cast doubt on the claim of cure.) After all, acute leukemia is counted an absolutely mortal disease, but a diligent search of the literature will turn up a small handful of cases of people who have had complete and lasting remission of acute leukemia. Why? No one knows. The analysts who claim that patients once alcoholic were later able to resume social, controlled drinking of course try to explain why in terms of the psychodynamics of the case. But until a number of such cures can be substantiated, we will have no reason to hold out any real hope for the complete cure of the alcoholic.

Nor—and here is the point—does it seem to us that talk of such a "cure" is pertinent or meaningful. Alcohol is a drug. It is a toxic drug. It performs certain useful functions for society as a whole, and for a large number of people it constitutes a pleasant ingredient in a beverage. But surely it is incorrect to say that he is a completely well person who is able to drink a toxic drug without doing himself damage. It would seem more correct to say he is a completely well person who, understanding why once he needed such a toxic drug to get along in life, now no longer has any slightest desire to depend on it.

The completely healthy man—physically, mentally, and emotionally—is the man who needs to repose no reliance on a drug. So to speak of *cure* in the sense of being able to resume such reliance safely is to hold out a very untrustworthy goal.

The goal we should aim for is a society in which there will be more of us sufficiently free of tension, sufficiently capable of amity and love for our fellows, that drugs will be confined to the medicine shelf. In such a society reality could be so pleasant that there would be no need to seek a temporary euphoria.

Sources of Help

For the alcoholic, the achievement of insight into the nature of his difficulty is, more often than not, a slow and painful process, one which he may resist implacably. So it is, likewise, with his wife and family. Thus it may happen that a man or woman may be quite patently an alcoholic but will flatly refuse to seek treatment in a clinic or assistance at a meeting of Alcoholics Anonymous. In recognition of this fact, we are listing here two quite different sorts of sources of help for the alcoholic. In the first group are Information Centers, organized and administered by local committees of the National Committee on Alcoholism (2 East 103rd Street, New York 29, N. Y.). These Information Centers maintain up-to-date information on local resources, working with doctors, clergymen, teachers, worried citizens, families and friends of alcoholics, or their employers. No treatment is given the alcoholic at these centers; here he will find only a friendly explanation or interpretation of his problems; from here he will be referred to a hospital, or to a doctor, or to a clinic, or to A.A. But here, very importantly, he will find a warm and sympathetic reception, and a valuable way-station on his way to clearer insight.

CALIFORNIA

Eden Committee on Alcoholism
594 Castro Street, Room 211   Hayward, Calif.

Monterey Peninsula C.E.A.
135 West Franklin Street   Monterey, Calif.

Pasadena Committee on Alcoholism
263 South Los Robles Avenue   Pasadena, Calif.

Santa Barbara Committee on Alcoholism
804 Santa Barbara Street   Santa Barbara, Calif.

DISTRICT OF COLUMBIA

Washington C.E.A.
2001 Kalorama Road   Washington, D. C.

ILLINOIS

Alton-Wood River Alcoholism Information Bureau
204½ State Street   Alton, Ill.

Chicago Committee on Alcoholism
743 North Wabash   Chicago 11, Ill.

MASSACHUSETTS

Boston Committee on Alcoholism
419 Boylston Street, Room 525   Boston 16, Mass.

Worcester Committee on Alcoholism
5 Claremont Street   Worcester 3, Mass.

MICHIGAN

Detroit Committee on Alcoholism
Doctors' Building, 3919 John R Street   Detroit 1, Mich.

Flint Committee on Alcoholism
402 Metropolitan Building   Flint, Mich.

NEW JERSEY

Essex County Committee on Alcoholism
120 Evergreen Place   East Orange, N. J.

NEW YORK

Broome County Committee on Alcoholism
443 O'Neill Building   Binghamton, N. Y.

Rochester Committee on Alcoholism
973 East Avenue   Rochester, N. Y.

Western New York C.E.A.
2183 Main Street   Buffalo, N. Y.

NORTH CAROLINA

Greensboro Citizens Committee on Alcoholism
Room 206, Irvin Arcade, 216 West Market Street   Greensboro,
N. C.

OHIO

Bureau on Alcoholism
212 West 12th Street   Cincinnati 10, Ohio

Youngstown Committee on Alcoholism
138 Lincoln Avenue   Youngstown, Ohio

PENNSYLVANIA

Bethlehem Committee on Alcoholism
7 East Church Street   Bethlehem, Pa.

Western Pennsylvania C.E.A.
220 Rose Street at Third Avenue   Pittsburgh, Pa.

TEXAS

Houston Committee on Alcoholism
1009 National State Building   Houston 2, Texas

Central West Virginia C.E.A.
204 Concord Street   Clarksburg, W. Va.

CANADA

Committee on Alcoholism for Manitoba
588 Broadway   Winnipeg, Manitoba

HAWAII

Hawaii Committee on Alcoholism
3627 Eilauea Avenue   Honolulu 16, T. H.

Additionally, several states have established official agencies to deal with public education and assistance in the field of alcoholism. These are: ALABAMA Commission on Education with Respect to Alcoholism, 408 Monroe Street, Montgomery; CONNECTICUT Commission on Alcoholism, 51 Coventry Street, Hartford 12; in DELAWARE, the Governor Bacon Health Center, Delaware City; DISTRICT OF COLUMBIA Department of Public Health, Alcoholic Rehabilitation Division, 2227 M Street, NW, Washington, D. C.; FLORIDA Alcoholic Rehabilitation Program, P.O. Box 665, Avon Park; GEORGIA Commission on Alcoholism, 1260 Briarcliff Road, NE, Atlanta; INDIANA Commission on Alcoholism, 1315 West Tenth Street, Indianapolis; KANSAS Commission on Alcoholism, 315 West Fourth Street, Topeka; LOUISIANA Commission on Alcoholism, Baton Rouge; MAINE Department of Health and Welfare, Division of Alcoholic Rehabilitation, State House, Augusta; MARYLAND Department of Health, Section on Alcohol Studies, 2411 North Charles Street, Baltimore 18; MASSACHUSETTS Department of Public Health, Division of Alcoholism, 8 Beacon Street, Boston; MICHIGAN Board of Alcoholism, 102 South

Walnut Street, Lansing; MINNESOTA Department of Health, University Campus, Minneapolis 14; MONTANA Board of Health, Narcotics and Alcoholism Program, Helena; NEW HAMPSHIRE Department of Health, Division on Alcoholism, 66 South Street, Concord; NEW JERSEY Department of Health, Bureau of Alcoholism Control, Trenton 7; NEW MEXICO Commission on Alcoholism, 116 East De Vargas, Santa Fe; NEW YORK Mental Health Commission, Alcoholism Program, 270 Broadway, New York 7; NORTH CAROLINA Alcoholic Rehabilitation Program, P.O. Box 9118, Raleigh; NORTH DAKOTA Commission on Alcoholism, 7A First Avenue, SW, Minot; OREGON Alcohol Education Committee, 808 Dekum Building, Portland 4; PENNSYLVANIA Department of Health, Division of Alcoholic Studies and Rehabilitation, Harrisburg; RHODE ISLAND Department of Social Welfare, Division of Alcoholism, 94 Doyle Avenue, Providence; UTAH Board on Alcoholism, 221 David Keith Building, Salt Lake City; VERMONT Alcoholic Rehabilitation Commission, 174 Pearl Street, Burlington; WISCONSIN Department of Public Welfare, Division of Mental Hygiene, Bureau of Alcohol Studies, 1552 University Avenue, Madison; VIRGINIA Department of Health, Division of Alcohol Studies and Rehabilitation, Richmond 19.

Finally, there are the out-patient clinics for alcoholics. Their number has grown in the past few years; indeed, there is every likelihood that this list is not complete, that still other clinics will have been launched before these lines are published.

These clinics may be supported by funds from state, county, or city government; they may be financed independently; they may receive support of local committees on alcoholism; but at each the alcoholic can obtain regular medical care, usually offered by both an internist and a psychiatrist.

Men's Service Club
541 East Fifth Street   Los Angeles 13, Calif.

Medical B, Pasadena Dispensary
38 Congress Street   Pasadena, Calif.

Adult Guidance Center
150 Otis Street   San Francisco 3, Calif.

Mary Young Memorial Clinic
804 Santa Barbara Street   Santa Barbara, Calif.

COLORADO

Cambio Clinic
Denver General Hospital, West Sixth Avenue and Cherokee
   Street   Denver 4, Colo.

"A" Clinic
4200 East Ninth Avenue   Denver, Colo.

CONNECTICUT

Commission on Alcoholism Clinic
Suite 406, Warner Building, 83 Fairfield Avenue   Bridgeport,
   Conn.

Blue Hills Hospital
51 Coventry Street   Hartford, Conn.

Commission on Alcoholism Clinic
51 Coventry Street   Hartford, Conn.

Commission on Alcoholism Clinic
412 Orange Street   New Haven, Conn.

Yale Plan Clinic
52 Hillhouse Avenue   New Haven, Conn.

Commission on Alcoholism Clinic
159 Main Street   Stamford, Conn.

Commission on Alcoholism Clinic
167 Grove Street   Waterbury, Conn.

Alcoholic Clinic
Governor Bacon Health Center   Delaware City, Del.

DISTRICT OF COLUMBIA

Alcoholic Rehabilitation Clinic
2227 M Street, NW   Washington, D. C.

FLORIDA

Alcoholic Rehabilitation Clinic
1241 South McDuff Avenue   Jacksonville, Fla.

Alcoholic Rehabilitation Clinic
Baptist Hospital,   Pensacola, Fla.

Alcoholic Rehabilitation Clinic
1303 Miccosukee Road   Tallahassee, Fla.

Alcoholic Rehabilitation Clinic
Professional Arts Building, Tampa, Fla.

Alcoholic Rehabilitation Clinic
1637 N.W. Tenth Avenue   Miami, Fla.

GEORGIA

The Georgian Clinic
1260 Briarcliff Road, N.E.   Atlanta, Ga.

Commission on Alcoholism Clinic
Wilhenford Building   Augusta, Ga.

ILLINOIS

Portal House
743 North Wabash   Chicago 11, Ill.

LOUISIANA

Alcoholic Treatment Center
Charity Hospital of Louisiana   New Orleans, La.

Medicine Clinic
Huey P. Long Charity Hospital   Pineville, La.

MARYLAND

Anne Arundel County Alcoholic Rehabilitation Clinic
Cathedral and South Streets   Annapolis, Md.

Washington County Alcoholic Rehabilitation Clinic
Washington County Health Center   Hagerstown, Md.

Montgomery County Alcoholic Rehabilitation Clinic
Jefferson Street   Rockville, Md.

Wicomico County Alcoholic Rehabilitation Clinic
Watson Memorial Building, West Locust Street   Salisbury, Md.

Baltimore County Alcoholic Rehabilitation Clinic
Susquehanna and Washington Streets   Towson 4, Md.

MASSACHUSETTS

Alcoholic Clinic, Massachusetts General Hospital
Fruit Street   Boston 14, Mass.

Alcoholic Clinic, Peter Bent Brigham Hospital
721 Huntington Avenue   Boston 15, Mass.

Re-Education Clinic, New England Hospital
Dimock Street   Roxbury, Mass.

Washingtonian Hospital
39 Morton Street, Jamaica Plain   Boston 18, Mass.

Brockton Thursday Nite Club
47 West Elm Street   Brockton, Mass.

Brockton Clinic for Alcoholism
Brockton Hospital   Brockton, Mass.

Brookline Committee on Alcoholism Clinic
10 Walter Avenue   Brookline 46, Mass.

St. Luke's Hospital
Taber Street   New Bedford, Mass.

Clinic for Alcoholism
Pittsfield General Hospital, 741 North Street   Pittsfield, Mass.

Clinic for Alcoholism
Quincy City Hospital, 114 Whitwell Street   Quincy, Mass.

Worcester City Hospital Psychosomatic Clinic
Out-Patient Department, Chandler Street   Worcester, Mass.

Alcoholic Clinic, St. Vincent Hospital
25 Winthrop Street   Worcester, Mass.

MICHIGAN

Detroit Committee on Alcoholism Clinic
Doctors' Building, 3919 John R Street   Detroit 1, Mich.

Mayor's Rehabilitation Committee on "Skid Row" Problems
672 East Woodbridge Street   Detroit 26, Mich.

MINNESOTA

Twin Cities Follow-Up Clinic
Mental Health Unit, 1111 Nicollet Avenue, Room 220   Minneapolis 3, Minn.

Duluth Follow-Up Clinic
Miller Memorial Hospital   Duluth, Minn.

Alcoholic Service Center
Wilder Dispensary, 279 Rice Street   St. Paul, Minn.

Twin Cities Follow-Up Clinic
St. Paul Office, Department of Public Welfare, 117 University Avenue   St. Paul, Minn.

NEW HAMPSHIRE

Division on Alcoholism Clinic
66 South Street   Concord, N. H.

NEW JERSEY

Study Clinic, West Jersey Hospital
Mt. Ephraim and Atlantic Avenue   Camden, N. J.

Study Clinic, St. Michael's Hospital
306 High Street Newark, N. J.

Study Clinic, McKinley Hospital
Brunswick Avenue Trenton, N. J.

Alcoholism Rehabilitation Center
Overlook Hospital, 103 Morris Avenue Summit, N. J.

Study Clinic, Passaic General Hospital
350 Boulevard Passaic, N. J.

NEW YORK

Broome County Committee on Alcoholism Out-Patient Clinic
Binghamton City Hospital, 25 Park Avenue Binghamton, N. Y.

State University Alcohol Clinic
Kings County Hospital, 606 Winthrop Street Brooklyn 3, N. Y.

Information and Rehabilitation Center for Alcoholics
Chronic Disease Research Institute, University of Buffalo, 2183
  Main Street Buffalo, N. Y.

International Clinic
135 West 125th Street New York 27, N. Y.

Silkworth Memorial Clinic
Knickerbocker Hospital, 70 Convent Avenue New York, N. Y.

University Hospital Clinic
303 East 20th Street New York, N. Y.

Alcoholism Treatment and Research Center, Home Term Court
300 Mulberry Street New York 12, N. Y.

Rochester Clinic for the Diagnosis and Treatment of Alcoholism
The Health Bureau, 44 Marshall Street Rochester 7, N. Y.

Rochester Clinic for the Diagnosis and Treatment of Alcoholism
Rochester General Hospital, Out-Patient Department, 501 Main
  Street, West Rochester, N. Y.

Alcoholism Service Division
Syracuse Dispensary, 610 East Fayette Street Syracuse, N. Y.

Mental Hygiene Clinic
Room 415, City Hall   Asheville, N. C.

Mental Hygiene Clinic
1618 Elizabeth Avenue   Charlotte, N. C.

North Carolina Memorial Hospital Clinic
School of Medicine, Psychiatric Treatment Center   Chapel Hill,
N. C.

Mental Hygiene Clinic
210 North Greene Street   Greensboro, N. C.

Keeley Out-Patient Clinic
403 West Washington Street   Greensboro, N. C.

Mental Hygiene Clinic
415 Halifax Street   Raleigh, N. C.

Alcoholic Clinic, Graylyn Hospital
Bowman Gray School of Medicine   Winston-Salem 7, N. C.

Clinic for Alcoholics
Forsyth County Health Department, North Woodland and
Seventh Street   Winston-Salem, N. C.

NORTH DAKOTA

North Dakota Commission on Alcoholism Clinic
7A First Avenue   Minot, N. D.

OHIO

The Alcoholism Clinic
Department of Psychiatry, Cincinnati General Hospital   Cincinnati 29, Ohio

Alcoholic Rehabilitation Center
Toledo Health Department, 635 North Erie Street   Toledo,
Ohio

Lincoln Avenue Alcoholic Clinic
138 Lincoln Avenue   Youngstown, Ohio

Oregon State Alcoholic Rehabilitation Clinic
808 Dekum Building   Portland 4, Ore.

City-County Clinic in Johnstown, Inc.
Johnstown, Cambria County, Pa.

Allentown Counseling Center for Alcoholism
Allentown Hospital, Seventeenth and Chew Streets   Allentown,
Pa.

State Rehabilitation Center for Alcoholism
Clarks Summit State Hospital   Clarks Summit, Pa.

Erie Counseling Center for Alcoholism
Hamot Hospital   Erie, Pa.

Counseling Center for Alcoholism
701 North Sixth Street   Harrisburg, Pa.

Philadelphia Counseling Center for Alcoholism
Sanatorium No. 4, Girard and Corinthian Avenues   Philadelphia,
Pa.

Alcoholism Unit, Philadelphia General Hospital, 34th and Curie
Avenues   Philadelphia, Pa.

C. Dudley Saul Clinic
St. Luke's and Children's Medical Center, Franklin and Thomp-
son Streets   Philadelphia 22, Pa.

Alcoholic Information Center and Clinic
200 Ross Street, Room 301   Pittsburgh 19, Pa.

Nutrition Clinic of Falk Clinics, University of Pittsburgh
3601 Fifth Avenue   Pittsburgh 13, Pa.

Staunton Clinic
3601 Fifth Avenue   Pittsburgh, Pa.

St. Francis Hospital
45th Street   Pittsburgh, Pa.

St. Margaret's Hospital
46th and Geneva Streets   Pittsburgh, Pa.

Newport Clinic
Trinity Church Parish House, High Street   Newport, R. I.

Doyle Avenue Clinic
94 Doyle Avenue   Providence 6, R. I.

TEXAS

Alcoholic Clinic, Jefferson Davis Hospital
1801 Buffalo Drive   Houston, Texas

Alcoholic Clinic, St. Joseph's Hospital
1910 Crawford Street   Houston, Texas

Alcoholic Clinic, Methodist Hospital
6516 Bertner Street   Houston, Texas

VERMONT

Alcoholic Clinic, Alcoholic Rehabilitation Commission
174 Pearl Street   Burlington, Vt.

Clinic, Alcoholic Rehabilitation Commission
19 Kingman Street   St. Albans, Vt.

VIRGINIA

Alexandria Health Department Alcoholic Clinic
517 North St. Asaph Street   Alexandria, Va.

Arlington County Guidance Center
1800 North Edison Street   Arlington, Va.

Division of Alcohol Studies and Rehabilitation
Department of Health, Medical College of Virginia, 1200 East
   Broad Street   Richmond, Va.

Alcoholic Clinic, Division of Alcohol Studies and Rehabilitation
Roanoke Public Health Center, Eighth and Campbell Avenue,
   S.W.   Roanoke, Va.

Alcoholic Treatment Center
1954 East Washington Avenue   Madison, Wis.

Alcoholic Clinic, Milwaukee County Dispensary
2430 West Wisconsin Avenue   Milwaukee 3, Wis.

Wausau Alcoholic Information Center
125 West Washington Street   Wausau, Wis.

CANADA

Alcoholism Foundation of Alberta Clinic
9910 103rd Street   Edmonton, Alberta

Alcoholism Foundation of Alberta Clinic
737–13 Avenue West   Calgary, Alberta

Alcoholism Foundation of British Columbia Clinic
1690 West Broadway   Vancouver, British Columbia

London Clinic
287 Queens Avenue   London, Ontario

Brookside Clinic
9 Bedford Road   Toronto, Ont.

Ottawa Clinic
185 Metcalfe Street   Ottawa, Ont.

Bell Clinic
15 Horsham Avenue   Willowdale, Ont.

Alcoholism Clinic, Allan Memorial Institute
1025 Pine Avenue, West   Montreal, Quebec

Alcoholic Clinic
Queen Elizabeth Hospital, 2100 Marlowe Avenue   Montreal,
   Quebec